FORENSIC DENTAL EVIDENCE: AN INVESTIGATOR'S HANDBOOK

First Edition

FORENSIC DENTAL EVIDENCE: AN INVESTIGATOR'S HANDBOOK

First Edition

C. Michael Bowers

ELSEVIER
ACADEMIC
PRESS

Amsterdam   Boston   Heidelberg   London   New York   Oxford
Paris   San Diego   San Francisco   Singapore   Sydney   Tokyo

Permissions may be sought directly from Elsevier's Science & Technology Rights Department in Oxford, UK: phone: (+44) 1865 843830, fax: (+44) 1865 853333, e-mail: permissions@elsevier.co.uk. You may also complete your request on-line via the Elsevier homepage (http://www.elsevier.com), by selecting 'Customer Support' and then 'Obtaining Permissions'

Elsevier Academic Press
525 B Street, Suite 1900, San Diego, California 92101-4495, USA
http://www.elsevier.com

Elsevier Academic Press
84 Theobald's Road, London WC1X 8RR, UK
http://www.elsevier.com

Library of Congress Catalog Number:
Bowers, C. Michael
Forensic dental evidence: an investigator's handbook – 2nd ed.
1. Dental jurisprudence
I. Title
614.1

British Library Cataloguing in Publication Data
A catalogue record for this book is available from the British Library

Cover images generated by Ray Johansen

ISBN 0-1212-1042-1

Printed and bound in Meppel, The Netherlands by Krips bv
03 04 05 06 07 08 9 8 7 6 5 4 3 2 1

To my family:
Cynthia, Kirstin and Jake

CONTENTS

CONTRIBUTORS

CONTRIBUTING AUTHORS

Dean Hildebrand, Vancouver, British Columbia, Canada
Raymond Johansen, Santa Barbara, CA
Ron O'Halloran, Ventura, CA
Duane Spencer, Walnut Creek, CA
Diane Penola, New York, NY
Michel Perrier, Lausanne, Switzerland
Iain Pretty, Liverpool, England
Michael Saks, Prescott, AZ

PHOTO CREDITS

Doug Arendt, Oakton, VA
Armed Forces Institute of Pathology
Art Burns, Jacksonville, FL
Gary Bell, Seattle, WA
Kelly Faddis, Orem, UT
Forensic Imaging Services, Santa Barbara, CA
Greg Golden, Los Angeles, CA
Dean Hildebrand, British Columbia, Canada
Ron O'Halloran, Ventura, CA
Helen James, Adelaide, Australia
Raymond Johansen, Santa Barbara, CA
Cathy Law, Los Angeles, CA
Lightning Powder, Inc.
Barry Lipton, Largo, FL
John McDowell, Denver, CO
Michel Perrier, Lausanne, Switzerland
Iain Pretty, Liverpool, England
Richard Souviron, Coral Gables, FL

Duane Spencer, Walnut Creek, CA
Jane Taylor, Adelaide, Australia
Mike Tabor, Nashville, TN
Gerald L. Vale, Los Angeles, CA
West Publishing Co.
James Wood, Cloverdale, CA

This book's purpose is to act as a detailed overview of forensic dentistry as it is practiced in the 21st century and contains presentations of dental investigation methods. Law enforcement and legal professionals are, in the end result, the clients of the dental expert. This book is written for this audience. Wherever possible, the author has included casework examples to explain the multiple areas that a forensic dentist can interact with police investigations. The reconstruction of prior events at a crime scene and individual's activities is a daunting task. Forensic examiners use dental evidence in this process. Certain suggestions and guidelines are described to raise the certainty of successfully recognizing and capturing vital dental evidence in actual forensic casework.

Development of modern forensic dentistry is seen in the dental and forensic literature over the last 50 years. Many of these cases are valuable for the innovative problem-based dental techniques used to compare known (K) and questioned (Q) dental evidence. They show considerable effort in answering questions asked by law enforcement and the courts. Interestingly, an independent body of forensic dental science didn't exist before dental identification and bite mark analysis became parts of contemporary forensic investigations. This follows the historical development of forensic pathology during the later 19th century period in Britain, France and Germany. Empirical studies in forensic dentistry do exist but still have not answered certain core questions involving human identification based on bite mark analysis that have been posed during the 21st century. The advent of DNA profiling and digital imaging are recent additions that are being used to increase the reliability of forensic dentists' bite mark opinions which previously used techniques that have varied only slightly for the last 40 years.

Apart from bite mark identification, the use of dental records and accompanying dental/medical radiographs to identify deceased individuals is a common event in the US and abroad that provides considerable assistance in mass disaster recoveries and cases identifying unknown persons. Beyond this broad overview, the need to properly identify and analyze dental evidence is an ongoing request made of dentists throughout the world. The transient nature of crime scene evidence places considerable pressure on law enforcement to immediately establish possible links between crime and its perpetrators. Mistakes and errors of evidence collection will never be properly remedied by later scientific manipulations in the crime laboratory.

In any criminal investigation, the proof of guilt or innocence is the underpinning focus of forensic efforts. Correct human identification of deceased individuals must be made to serve both law enforcement and surviving family members. It is just as important to eliminate a homicide or assault case suspect, as it is to strongly tip the scale of justice to charge a person of criminal conduct. The cases that are unclear as to guilt and innocence, or at least have weak connections between the crime scene and a suspect, rely even more heavily on physical evidence in order to give the justice system a chance to produce a reliable outcome. When the forensic dental evidence is clear and physically compelling, the truth seems obvious to the judicial system, judge and a lay jury. When the dental evidence is vague, ambiguous or otherwise equivocal, it is important for law enforcement and the forensic expert to honestly weigh the value of the evidence against the potential for irrevocable harm to a defendant.

The management of the physical evidence of a crime falls to a series of actors during the entire course of a case. The beginning phase has the managers generally being police staff at a scene. Occasionally the first collection of dental evidence is through the efforts of the forensic pathologist or forensic dentist during a postmortem examination. In a mass disaster, recovery of human remains should be the job of a trained civilian, military or government personnel. In all instances, the persons responsible for detecting, documenting and collecting the physical evidence are the gatekeepers for the process that follows. The management at any scene should be under the control of prepared experienced professionals. In the continuum of events after evidence recognition and collection, the forensic laboratory or forensic dentists will obtain control of the evidence and perform their analyses. These forensic opinions will be transferred to the legal arena where attorneys will introduce the evidence. Their duty will be to translate to their judicial audience the importance this evidence has to the case at hand.

THE LOGIC OF FORENSIC INVESTIGATION

Aspects of proper forensic evidence recovery requires a knowledge-base contained in the steps listed below:

- **Recognition (detection)**
  Teeth and related physical evidence derived from the oral cavity must be noticed by responding crime scene and accident investigators. These professionals must also be familiar with common objects that may contain transfer evidence such as

saliva or tooth impression evidence. These objects include human skin, clothing, duct tape, envelopes, chewing gum, telephone receivers, foods: such as cheese and various types of beverage containers.

- **Documentation (recording)**

  Physical evidence obtained from a crime or accident scene should be left in place, properly lighted and photographed. This establishes its condition and context with the location prior to investigative measures that may disturb or somehow alter its condition. The photographer must take the time to place size-reference scales or rulers in some of the evidence photos. This allows the pictures and the evidence to be later made life-size via photographic or digital processing. Written notes or log sheets with pertinent descriptions should be kept by the investigator responsible for the evidence collection.

- **Collection**

  The intent is to capture the dental evidence for later analysis. This commonly includes bagging biological objects (saliva stains, loose teeth or food stuffs) in labeled paper bags. Bite marks in skin, if seen on someone at a crime scene, should be rigorously photographed and then swabbed. Recreating the position or posture of the person bitten should be considered, but without a victim's statement or reliable witness, all alternatives should be considered.

- **Preservation**

  Protocols for the capture and preservation of biological evidence (tissue, blood, semen or saliva) must be stringently followed. Foodstuffs cannot be preserved for long periods of time without drying and deteriorating. The method of choice to preserve bite impressions in food is to take modeling impressions of the objects as soon as practical after swabbing for saliva. Bite marks in skin can be impressed with dental molding materials. This permits later creation of a three-dimensional model of the bitten area.

- **Interpretation**

  The recreation of a human's identity by their teeth or via DNA taken from a tooth or saliva requires scientific training and should be performed by a Board certified forensic dentist for the former, and biologist for the latter.

CATEGORIES OF DENTAL EVIDENCE

The various types of dental evidence can be described as they relate to questions being asked by the investigators.

"Is there direct dental evidence supporting human identification?"

Evidence types

- A human tooth or tooth fragment.
- A fragment of a human jawbone.

- DNA obtained from a tooth, toothbrush, cigarette, etc.
- DNA obtained from a swabbing of a bite mark, foodstuff or object that possesses saliva transfer evidence.
- Dental restorations and appliances that can be associated to a particular person through name inscriptions, specific dental material type, composition or unusual design characteristics.

"Is there associative evidence of a person's past presence or activities at a crime scene?". This type of question asked by investigators extends to:

- Does the bite mark in this apple indicate a specific person was present at a scene prior to or during the commission of a crime?
- Does the DNA obtained from this piece of bitten cheese belong to a specific person?
- Does the DNA obtained from the swabbing of this telephone belong to a specific person who was present at the scene?
- Can this "person of interest" be eliminated as a suspect?
- Does the suspect's statement of consensual sexual contact with the victim seem appropriate with the severity of this bite mark?

Transfer evidence corroboration

- Does the saliva obtained from a glass that also has fingerprint evidence contain the DNA of the same individual matching the fingerprints?

This book contains concepts and protocols vital to a successful outcome to a criminal investigation containing dental evidence. One basis for any proven forensic dental protocol is organization and regular utilization. These methods need to be practiced and protocols maintained in order to be available and successful under actual casework conditions.

It is my wish that this book will help improve the body of knowledge available on the uses and importance of dental evidence.

Dr. Mike Bowers
October 1, 2003
Ventura, California, USA
email: cmbowers@aol.com

ACKNOWLEDGEMENTS

The author wants to thank the following people, each a friend and a mentor, who have been instrumental in my arriving at this point in my professional career: Dr. Charles Meyer Goldstein for setting an incredibly high standard of community and humanitarian service during his 34 year career at USC; Dr. Gerald L. Vale, also at USC, who gave me my first glimpse of forensic dental investigation; Dr. Warren Lovell who provided the welcome that allowed my forensic science interest to develop and to Dr. Ron O'Halloran who continues in his place at the Ventura County Medical Examiner's Office. Finally, I have to thank Dr. Raymond Johansen for his dedicated interest in improving forensic dentistry and for his innovative spirit.

INTRODUCTION

Human identification is the *forensic odontologist's* primary duty. This involves inter-action with law enforcement agencies charged with the responsibility of inves-tigating the evidence from cases involving violent crime, child abuse, elder abuse, missing persons and mass disaster scenarios. In each context, dental evi-dence may produce compelling associations to aid victim identity, suspect iden-tity and also establish facts that can affect the direction and ultimate outcome of investigative casework. It is possible to use dental evidence to identify people present during the commission of a crime or witnesses to an accident. The Board Certified forensic dentist interacts with other forensic and medical dis-ciplines like anthropology, pathology, human anatomy and biological science. The American Board of Forensic Odontology (ABFO) oversees certification in the US and Canada. The ABFO is co-located with the American Academy of Forensic Sciences (AAFS), in Colorado Springs, Colorado, USA.

Forensic dentistry (aka forensic odontology in Europe) has a two and one half century history in the US. It is the science and practice of dentistry and its role in modern society. Dental injuries from accidents or assaults must be assessed and treated. Occasionally, the treating dentist or attending forensic dental expert testifies in court proceedings for parties involved in civil litigation. Criminal cases use dentists to testify on dental evidence obtained from a crime scene or crime victims. Occasionally, a perpetrator of a crime leaves evidence at a scene. Bitten food, gum or chewed objects may be recovered by law enforce-ment. Autopsy investigations may notice bite marks on the skin of a deceased victim. Dental experts also testify regarding the quality of dental care (profes-sional negligence) and in cases where dental fraud is an issue.

HISTORICAL BACKGROUND OF FORENSIC DENTISTRY

The seminal historical case in the US surrounded the identification by dental evidence of a senior American officer killed during the Battle of Breeds (Bunker)

Hill, in 1775. He died from a gunshot through his cheek that exited through the back of his head. This patriot, Dr. Joseph Warren, was buried in an unmarked grave by the victorious (but later vanquished) British forces. Ten months later, Warren's family attempted to recover his remains for a proper burial. The grave held two bodies. Paul Revere identified the body of Warren. Known for his American Revolutionary exploits, Revere was also a silversmith and occasional denture-maker. He accomplished the identification of one skeletal remains by recognizing a partial denture constructed by him for Dr. Warren. Revere had opened an office in 1768 for the practice of dentistry after receiving training from John Baker, an English surgeon dentist. These artificial teeth were a remarkable combination of silver wire and a portion of a hippopotamus tusk designed to replace a missing eyetooth. Dr. Warren was a graduate of Harvard University and a leader of the Sons of Liberty, a revolutionary organization that instigated anti-British activities such as the Boston Tea Party. Revere was more than just Warren's dentist. Warren sent Revere the dentist/silversmith on his famous ride to warn the militia about the approaching British forces. Warren was buried with full honors on April 8, 1776.

The Parkman murder of 1850 is the second notable odontology case in US forensic science. It involved dental evidence given at trial where a conviction was assisted by dental evidence. The testimony of Dr. Nathan Cooley Keep, later first dean of the Harvard School of Dentistry, was pivotal in identifying the murder victim. This case was the judicial precursor to modern criminal cases where the dental identification was linked with other facts to recreate the circumstances of the case. The dentist did not testify as to the defendant's guilt or innocence but positively stated who was the victim.

The defendant was Dr. John White Webster, a Professor at Harvard Medical School. His duties included lecturing in anatomical science and he had a laboratory at the Medical School. Dr. Webster was an overspending type and had run through both his inheritance and his $2,000 per annum salary when he started to borrow money from a Dr. George Parkman, a retired physician. Dr. Parkman sustained his income via money lending and was a sizable donor to Harvard College. The two doctors were acquaintances and Webster had used a valuable mineral collection as collateral for loans from Parkman amounting to a $2,432.

Webster mis-stepped in his financial dealings with Parkman by double dealing his mineral collection as collateral to another loan shark who, unfortunately for Webster, was an in-law of Parkman. Upon finding out of this double-dealing, Parkman quickly demanded reparations and threatened public humiliation for Webster's transgression. A meeting between the two was set for noon on Friday, November 23, 1849 with Webster promising appeasement. Parkman arrived at Webster's office next to the medical building, shortly before noon on the appointed time. He was never seen alive again.

One week later, a dutiful janitor found dismembered human remains in the outhouse behind Webster's office at the medical school. Portions of a porcelain denture as well as a crushed skull were recovered from a laboratory furnace.

The trail of the missing Dr. Parkman obviously led right to Webster. Disregarding his activities as an anatomist, who could legitimately dispose of bones in the furnace, the police must have suspected him as having some motives in having Parkman disappear.

The prominence of characters of this case created a publicity firestorm in Boston. Spectators at the trial were only given 10 minutes of time in the gallery. Newspapers heralded the case against Webster. A star witness for the prosecution was Dr. Keep. He had been Parkman's dentist for over 20 years and had constructed a porcelain denture one year before the murder. This same denture, actually numerous large fragments of it, were identified by Keep as belonging to Dr. Parkman. The dentist was so painstaking in his treatment that he still had the plaster model of Dr. Parkman's jaw and demonstrated to the jury its fit with the denture.

Dr. Webster was convicted of murder, sentenced to hang, lost an appeal and was executed in 1850. He confessed to the crime on the eve of his demise.

Contemporary practitioners of forensic dentistry in the US owe considerable thanks to dentists from the mid 20th century who established the ABFO and the British, Australian and European professional organizations that foster training excellence and standards of practice for dentists who work in this field. Their example of self-sacrifice and commitment to the establishment of forensic dentistry cannot be ignored.

LAW ENFORCEMENT INVESTIGATORS AND FORENSIC DENTAL EVIDENCE

The crime scene will seldom have a dentist as a first responder to the scene nor will one respond with the forensic evidence team or with major crime or detective bureau. Therefore, it is up to the police to perform the dental evaluations at a scene. The threshold question for any investigator at a crime scene or autopsy is "What is dental evidence?". This might seem to be begging the obvious but the purpose of this book is to clearly describe the gamut of evidence that is either directly related to human dental anatomy or derived from the oral environment. The survivability of teeth in catastrophic conditions is the feature that makes forensic odontologists regular participants in the autopsy suite. Tooth shapes, appearances, tooth fragments, metal restorations, skull and jawbone fragments may possess features that can be associated with just one person. The robust identification value of DNA, obtained from the inside of teeth and oral fluids, has recently created an entirely new level of identification, the biomolecular identification of individuals. The association of tooth marks in skin (bite marks) or other substances to the physical tooth characteristics of suspects has always been a useful tool to *include* or *exclude* suspects and people under police investigation.

Knowledge, training and experience are the keys to successful law enforcement casework. Good luck in an investigation is really the effect of hard work, thoroughness and preparation. The purpose of this book is to provide the basis of knowledge and training in forensic odontology that will extend into crime scene investigations and the crime laboratory.

Evidence *identification, documentation, preservation* and *collection* are the steps in this process. Identification technicians, crime scene evidence technicians and investigators must achieve a functional knowledge and the necessary skills to connect this evidence to the case for later analysis by the certified odontologist. The evidence collection process includes knowing the physical parameters of dental evidence that demand special steps in preservation before transportation to the crime lab. If the evidence is properly identified, collected, preserved and finally *transported*, it is also critical that the investigator properly document these steps to insure *authentication* and *chain of custody* for all interested parties. The success of later evidence analysis, whether *direct physical evidence* or even *circumstantial evidence*, is directly related to what happens during these first steps.

Specialized materials and methods are used to collect certain types of dental evidence. It is also important for the investigator to know what happens to evidence once it is transported to the forensic technician or forensic odontologist. In that regard, the later section of this book will demonstrate specialized collection techniques, materials, photographic documentation and analytical steps involved in laboratory processing and later comparison of physical and biological dental evidence.

EDUCATIONAL OBJECTIVES

Completing this book should provide the reader with the following knowledge and skills.

- The ability to identify types of dental evidence. This includes the various transfer surfaces and materials that may capture dental evidence.
- Appreciate the forensic identification significance and limitations of these categories of dental evidence.
- Properly document, collect and preserve these categories of dental physical and biological evidence.
- Knowledge of dental materials and supplies associated with evidence collection and preservation.
- Understand the judicial requirements regarding evidence collection, storage, and chain of custody.
- Develop a familiarity with digital comparison techniques via Adobe Photoshop®.

CHAPTER 1

DENTAL DETECTIVES

WHO IS A QUALIFIED FORENSIC DENTIST? ADVICE: USE THE BEST

Outside of the US military and federal government forensic units, there are no full time dentists doing forensic odontology in the US. Most investigators will have to retain an "outside" dentist as a case forensic consultant. This will be a serious step in the investigation. There are numerous referral agencies for forensic experts but law enforcement should be aware of some background information regarding the discipline. The US and Canada have a total of 84 Board Certified (American Board of Forensic Odontology, www.abfo.org) forensic dentists. These individuals have completed a constellation of prerequisite training in contrast to numerous self-taught or self-certified dentists who might also be considered for participation as a consultant. The ABFO requires formalized forensic coursework at either the Armed Forces Institute of Pathology, the University of Texas at San Antonio School of Dentistry or approved equivalent organizations. The *diplomates* of the ABFO are members of the American Academy of Forensic Sciences (www.aafs.org, an organization of 50 years of forensic excellence) who must sit for a three-day ABFO examination. This exam includes oral case examination, practical forensic testing in dental and bite mark identification, clinical dental pathology and ethical considerations in forensic science. The prerequisites to sit the exam include a formal affiliation with a medico-legal agency (this generally is a consultant's role with a Coroner or Medical Examiner's office), 25 completed cases of dental identification and 2 bite mark cases that are submitted for ABFO review prior to the examination. Bite mark casework, in particular, requires the applicant to have experience as the principal investigator for evidence collection during autopsy and/or sexual assault exams. It should be noted that the AAFS currently has 425 members of the Odontology (dentistry) section, indicating that those also ABFO certified are in the minority. The distribution of ABFO diplomates is scattered throughout the US with New York and California having the largest contribution. The majority of other States have at least one or two diplomates. Canada has five diplomates. As a final kudo, the vast majority of published papers, articles and books on forensic dentistry in the US have ABFO members either as authors, editors or major contributors.

A critical point arises when a death or major crimes investigator determines that a forensic dentistry expert is needed for a particular case. This book provides an overview on forensic dentistry but somewhere in the case, sooner better than later, a qualified dentist should be called. The numbers described above clearly show that agencies outside major metropolitan areas of the US and Canada may not have easy access to ABFO members. The question "Why should we use an ABFO diplomate?" is the next decision-making step for the investigator. The informed investigator should know that more complicated the identification cases have the best results when an experienced dental expert is used. Statistical studies have proven that dentists with little to no formalized forensic training have less accurate results in complicated casework. The investigator has to also ask "Is this a complicated or a simple identification case?" Certainly any bite mark case should include a dentist as soon as possible in the investigation who has the skill, training and experience to assess the value of this type of evidence and perform appropriate analyses. The simpler case of identifying a deceased subject from dental records may be within the realm of any licensed dentist but the investigator should value the use of an ABFO diplomate for a second opinion whenever possible. This does not reflect negatively on those dentists who are developing their forensic skills. This caution is based on the fact that formal undergraduate and postgraduate training in forensic dentistry is not consistent throughout North America.

WHAT DENTISTS DO

Hospital emergency room personnel, law enforcement, District Attorneys, Coroners and Medical Examiner agencies frequently develop cases that require dental expertise. The criminal defense bar also uses certified forensic dentists to review and analyze evidence relevant to judicial proceedings. The realm of the forensic dentist crosses into all aspects of criminal investigation. The most common cases are missing and unidentified persons (MUPs) cases where there are unidentified human remains found at a crime scene. Dental evidence becomes important for such human identification cases when fingerprints are not obtainable from decomposed or skeletonized remains. In the case of "fresh" human remains, the lack of personal effects (e.g. driver's license, credit card information, etc.) or surrounding circumstances (vehicle registration or known place of residence) can frustrate the first step in a case. This first step is the identification of who the person is. The recovery of US Congressional aide Chandra Levy's body in May 2002 required the services of a forensic dentist in order to identify her. The September 11, 2001 terrorist acts at the World Trade Center, the Pentagon and Pennsylvania required the efforts of hundreds of dentists, some Board Certified and others willing to help on-site to achieving the goal of identifying the victims. When conventional identification means are thwarted, dentistry is generally considered optimal when there is sufficient dental information before and after death. DNA profiling is used for severe body part fragmentation and where dental records are not available. Individual teeth obtained from a crime scene can be used to develop a DNA profile of an unidentified person. The dental nerve and root tissue can be analyzed by biochemical means to recover the person's DNA characteristics.

The second aspect of forensic dentistry is the recognition, documentation and preservation of bite mark evidence. Teeth marks can be found in food, gum, soft objects and on human skin. The former can be left at crime scenes; the later can be found on the bodies of assault victims, both dead and alive. The comparison of these teeth marks to a particular suspected person requires the services of an experienced forensic dentist. These evidence types also may contain saliva which is deposited on the object or skin during the act of biting or chewing. This saliva can be a rich source of DNA. Specific methods for collection will be covered later in Chapters 3 and 4.

Although dentistry is its own forensic specialty, it is important for the investigator to understand commonly used dental terminology and be able to recognize dental evidence. We will provide fundamental terms and descriptions of human adult and baby teeth in this chapter.

Cases are presented at the end of this chapter to illustrate how this information can be used to produce a positive investigative outcome.

WHAT TO DO WHEN "A SKULL WITH SOME TEETH" HAS BEEN DISCOVERED

The time to find a qualified forensic dentist is not when you get a phone call of a "found" skeleton with an intact skull in your jurisdiction. Begin in advance to develop a good working relationship with your dental expert before you need him or her. Since death and crime scene technicians are tasked with the duty to investigate known or suspected death scenes, you should be aware of the protocols and concepts surrounding the identification of human remains via dental means. The initial realization should be that it is paramount to initiate a thorough and well-documented trail of your investigative steps taken in the field. The material in this book will hopefully provide a backbone for investigators to develop their own protocols if none exist or determine that current ones need upgrading. The following indicates the general case conditions where a forensic dentist is needed as part of the investigation team when condition of the human remains is poor.

A call to a scene, where the first responder indicates a decomposed human skull, body or a clump of potentially human bones or burned fragments of bones, has to be both an exciting and challenging opportunity for any investigator. This is not the usual case where a fresh intact or partially intact body is present. Upon arrival, the investigator has to remember that many of the typical human identifiers may not be present. Burn victims seem totally devoid of human features. Fingerprints, definite body parameters of height and weight, eye color and hair color and the possibility of visual identification will be eradicated. There may be no available personal effects (wallet contents, passport, engraved jewelry, etc.). There are limits to assumptions regarding personal property found on or near a scene and they must be considered in the totality of other circumstantial and physical evidence. Caution must be exercised. The presence of distinctive tattoos on residual skin found on the body might be present but skin, although capable of becoming mummified in a proper dry and cool environment, may not be present after prolonged exposure to climatic elements or man-made (e.g. mutilation) conditions. Notable old surgical sites or significant medical history will have to be considered during autopsy and left to the realm of the Medical Examiner to value in comparison to personal history and medical records associated with a known individual.

The on-scene investigator should know five scenarios in which human remains require dental examination:

1. *Intact body with little to no decomposition found with no identification.* The general sequence of multi-discipline input in this case type has the dead person's fingerprints being taken by law enforcement and then uploaded to regional or national databases. The absence of personal effects will inhibit association of the body with local information. The absence of a timely missing person's report may inhibit developing leads. The dental exam should be done to allow maximum data collection early in the process.

2. *Decomposing human remains.* The possibility of fingerprints will be remote in this case. The use of dental information at the onset of the case may quickly add to the profile of the decedent and should be correlated with personal effects or outside information on identity.

3. *Skeletonized human remains.* Law enforcement in this scenario should use both a forensic dentist and a forensic anthropologist. Forensic anthropology is a specialty recognized by the AAFS. These individuals have special training in human osteology (bone science), excavation and recovery methods and analysis of bones for forensic information.

4. *High-energy accidents or terrorist acts.* These events cause severe trauma, dismemberment and fragmentation of human victims. The forensic team assigned to these cases must include a trained forensic dentist.

5. *Homicide cases.* The autopsy team should include a highly-trained forensic dentist to lend experience with analysis of bruises and marks on crime victims that may have been caused by teeth.

6. *Sexual assault and domestic violence cases.* Victims and suspects will bite in the course of a violent assault. The patterns produced by teeth in biting must be photographed and sometimes impressed for three-dimensional modeling by a trained technician or forensic dentist. The analysis of the pattern's possible link to a particular biter (i.e. bite mark identification) is dependent on proper evidence collection at the beginning of the case. An experienced forensic dentist should do this analysis.

These types of cases are difficult to quickly or even successfully reach the determination of human identity. This is where the forensic dentist is available for vital assistance to answer the important questions. The dentist can estimate age of the deceased, help reconstruct the person's dental profile and run out leads of potential identities using dental comparison techniques. The dentist can indicate whether the person was dentally healthy or showed sings of self-neglect or indigence. The dentist will also note indicators of the person's appearance. In bite mark identification, answers may be provided as to the appearance of a specific bite pattern in skin or foreign object recovered from a crime scene. In all scenarios listed above, it is paramount that the forensic dentist be included in the process from the very first phase in order to optimize results. An incident that has the potential for large amounts of human remains should have a dentist in the disaster plan to assist in the discovery and recovery phases. There will only be one chance to properly process such a scene. A dentist's familiarity with highly fragmented dental and human remains will accelerate the recovery process and help organize the identification process at the morgue or laboratory.

Besides the environmental factors that work to destroy, distort or diminish the physical characteristics of a deceased body, there may be animal or insect activity that will further degrade the evidence. Fully skeletonized remains require specific steps in insuring preservation of the human material. The chances of compromising an investigation increase exponentially with the decrease in available forensic information. The steps at the scene must center on preservation of obvious human material and a thorough review of the surface underlying the body part, be it solid ground, brush, gravel or a muddy-stream bed.

Investigators need to know *why* a person died. *Who* that person is allows them to backtrack to *where* the person was last seen or known to be alive. Without the *who*, there is no *where* for the case to go unless a missing persons report is filed in the same jurisdiction, a nearby jurisdiction, or a jurisdiction that is networked with a functioning and reliable area or national database. *When* the person died is important as well. Case investigators should consider experts of entomology, pathology and other fields in attempting to reconstruct time since death. The dentist can provide the *who* portion of the puzzle.

All of the above lists many factors that are not controlled by the investigator. Other people at the scene, the murderer, the weather, etc., take their toll on the outcome. The investigator, conversely, has total control over the scene upon arrival. The specific areas of control that must be maximized are:

1. Control your assumptions regarding the *who, why,* and *how* and wait longer than you feel is necessary to answer those burning questions. Once stated, they are very hard to erase if wrong. Outside pressures from media, supervisors, politicians, etc. may seem to be overwhelming for an impressionable investigator. To counter this, just keep in mind how bad your feelings and other sensibilities will be if you mis-identify the deceased.

2. An equivocal crime scene (could be a natural death or could be a homicide or an accident) must be initially treated as a homicide. There is no way to recover from making a mistake at this stage of the activities. You cannot back up if the scene is released too early because of a mistake. Evidence will be lost.

3. The overall conditions of the scene will determine what kind of plan you must have to recover the remains and its associated evidence. For example, a scene initially investigated outdoors at night should be thoroughly processed during the day. A wet and marshy area will take special equipment to control moisture and bacterial contamination of trace evidence. Burned human remains in an incinerated car will require a thorough search of the vehicle for lost teeth (very fragile and brittle) and metal dental restorations (they may be partially melted). Honestly assess your personnel and equipment resources and be flexible regarding what your plan's limitations may be. If possible, think backwards from the final location of the evidence (crime lab or autopsy suite) to the crime scene's original location of the evidence. This will create a better awareness of what needs to be done at the scene. Write your plan using these steps. If you still have questions, ask for help from people who have more experience in successful scene analysis before you process the scene.

4. The documentation of the scene should include all the basics including written notes, drawings with measurements and mapping. This is done before removing any remains or evidence. Put dirt and material removed from around the remains in a specific neutral place near the scene to allow the possibility of a future return and re-evaluation. This does not mean throwing the dirt in close proximity to the body over a cliff. Carefully remove it and put it in a safe place. Ground underneath the remains should be sifted. Tag all objects, photograph

and map before removal. Take orientation photographs of the general scene showing these tags before bagging individual pieces of evidence.

5. Consider how a perpetrator or accomplice may have entered and left the scene, before transporting the remains.
6. Take each step very slowly.
7. An experienced forensic dentist could answer specific questions about dental evidence present at a scene.

Concepts involving recovery of dental remains should concentrate on all of the above, in addition to the following concerns:

1. Teeth are small and may be broken into smaller pieces by high-energy impacts (aircraft or car crash).
2. Burned or incinerated teeth are extremely fragile. After documentation, the investigator should spray the tooth with a clear lacquer to help stabilize the ashen tooth structure before removal.
3. Bitten objects must be carefully collected and placed in paper bags that are properly labeled. This type of packaging lessens the chance of bacterial growth on the object, which may inhibit later recovery of salivary DNA at the lab.
4. Metal dental work may be misshapen due to heat damage. Gold crowns will look gray or black and metal partial dentures can appear twisted and blackened.
5. Bite marks on skin may look like round or almost circular bruises. The investigator must look for a series of small bruises or cuts that are arranged in a half-circular shape. Many times upper and lower teeth will not be apparent, just one or the other. Some object blocking one jaw from marking the skin causes this; usually it is clothing of the victim.

THE USE OF TEETH BY FORENSIC SCIENCE

The investigator should know the human species, in periods of development from child to adult, possesses at different stages 20 deciduous (baby teeth) and 32 adult teeth. Some of this total complement of 52 teeth may be present in a 1-year-old infant or a 90-year-old person. There is a transition period during the ages of about 6–12 years where adult teeth and deciduous teeth are both present. Twelve is the average age where all deciduous teeth are gone and the adult teeth are present. Wisdom teeth (third molars), if present, may start erupting into the oral cavity at the age of 18.

Teeth may also tell a story. In a real sense, there is a dental profile that can be developed from a person's mouth and teeth. Some teeth can give us an idea of racial characteristics. Asian and native American populations can have upper front teeth that are scooped out in back (aka shovel-shaped incisors). Teeth can tell us if an unidentified person was lucky enough to have their teeth straightened as a child or as an adult. Orthodontic work in the US commonly includes the removal of four bicuspids in order to perform teeth straightening. This also indicates a certain social status or income level since orthodontics is usually an elective procedure. Old dental fillings, using gold, show the person has received dental work over many years. New dental fillings show recent visits to a dentist. Whitened teeth and white caps show the person was concerned about their appearance and had financial resources to receive cosmetic dental work. Gold fillings and caps also show the person could afford expensive dental care. Large silver fillings show less expensive dental care was received. Decayed or missing teeth can tell the person was not getting regular dental care. Stainless steel or chrome caps are more economical than fancy porcelain (glass covered) caps and white fillings. Certain dental metals and materials are used and traceable to geographic regions or countries. Cells in the nerves and roots of undamaged teeth possess the biological makeup (DNA) of an individual. Even teeth fragments may allow investigators to determine an individual's DNA code via genetic testing. The sex of the person is proven by the presence or absence of a Y chromosome (male feature) in a tooth's genetic profile.

The comparison of past X-rays and dental records to the dental features of an unknown dead person is the primary step in dental identification. Finding these old records (both dental and medical) is vital for a completion of any identification case. Communication between the 50 States and the FBI missing person's archive (National Crime Information Centre, NCIC) must be improved regarding missing persons. To this date, most missing person's reports in the US do not include dental information.

FACTORS THAT CHANGE THE APPEARANCE OF TEETH OVER A LIFETIME

Dentistry has been a component of human history for eons. The development of *Homo sapiens* from its *primate* predecessors eventually introduced new pressures on the health and well-being of earth's inhabitants. The diet and habits of early man created increased wear and tear on teeth and the supporting dental structures of the jaw. Rustic means of grain production produced very abrasive foodstuffs due to incorporation of fine grit. This accelerated attrition and later breakage of child and adult teeth. Figures 1.1–1.3 show teeth with severe wear caused by dietary habits.

Modern civilization during the last two millennia improved on food production for the segments of society who could afford more refined food. The introduction of sugar and finely milled flour or maize increased the prevalence of tooth decay in these populations. This results in a dental profile much different from primitive society.

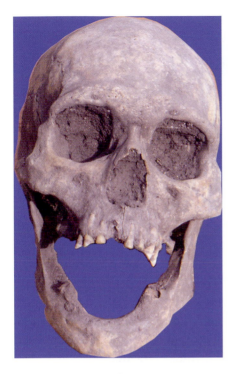

Figure 1.1

This is an "ancient" skull that was embedded in layers of hardened mud at a depth of 2–3 feet. This indicates a significant time passage since its burial. It was found during a construction excavation and had no accompanying evidence. Supporting this opinion is the severe dental attrition (tooth wear) and the skull being thoroughly desiccated (dried out) and mineralized over time. A "fresh" skeletonized or partially decomposed skull would have a much smoother bony surface and an obvious odor of "rotten eggs".

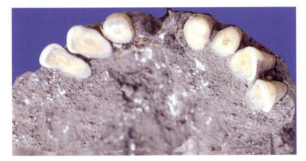

Figure 1.2

Close-up view of upper front teeth from the excavated skull. The extent of wear seen in "modern" teeth is much less. In this specimen, all the enamel on the chewing surfaces has been worn away, resulting in exposed root material. The dental nerve or "pulp chamber" in these teeth appear as circular or ovoid areas in the center of each tooth.

Contemporary dentistry has thrived on the existence of tooth decay and tooth loss. The efforts to reconstruct natural teeth that have been lost are recorded in ancient history from Egypt to the present. In modern times the presence of dental restorations and a history of dental treatment can allow investigators to identify deceased human remains. Forensic cases for human identification actually contain multiple specialists. Finger print experts, forensic anthropologists, DNA technicians, crime scene technicians, pathologists and

Figure 1.3

Close-up view of the skull's molar (chewing teeth) showing severe wear. This wear process may sometimes lead to severe dental abscess formation. These infections cause large amount of bone destruction adjacent to the offending teeth.

dentists all may have a part in rebuilding the circumstances of a person's demise as well as who that person is.

These man-made changes to the human dentition are a foundation for the modern identification of individuals. This investigative profiling focuses on dental work, medical devices, skull features and tooth changes that have occurred during their lives. These features are memorialized in photographs, dental and head X-rays and other medical imaging methods produced during a person's life. The assumption is that these features (both natural and man-made) are sufficiently unusual in their totality to make a determination of "possible, probable or a positive" identification. One should realize that a determination less than "positive" means the body could be someone else.

A negative (i.e. exclusionary) finding is obtained when features are considered dissimilar (no match) or in harder cases where they are similar but are not the same specific two-dimensional shape. In all dental identification cases, the comparisons must be made using X-rays or other radiographic representations of the before and after death dental features. Cases that simply use before death written medical and dental records for comparisons can never be as certain. The first commandment for the investigator should be *always obtain X-ray records* if there is a possibility of their existence. The following case involved a murdered teenager whose body was encased in a cement-filled barrel and dumped. The remains were recovered weeks after the murder and technicians were unable to recover fingerprints from the remains. There was significant circumstantial evidence pointing to who the body was but dental records were used to confirm the identification (Figure 1.4). This is commonly done when there is adequate dental evidence as it is faster and cheaper than DNA analysis.

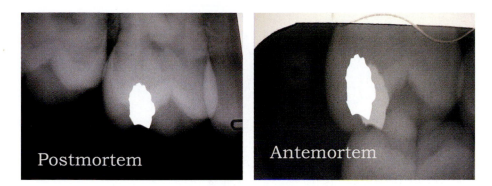

Figure 1.4

Two dental X-rays from an actual identification case. A metal filling in the left X-ray (Postmortem) appears as a white shape. The right X-ray (Antemortem) was obtained from a missing girl's dental records that were over 10 years old. The tooth with the filling in both X-rays is an adult molar that was filled with a metal restoration. Digital computer correction was then performed to make both images similar in dimensional shape. Finally, the outline of the upper filling was digitally transferred onto the right X-ray for two-dimensional comparison. The shape similarities are sufficient to support a positive dental identification determination.

In the case of no dental evidence, DNA would probably be the first resort regarding the issue of identity.

THE LANGUAGE OF DENTAL IDENTIFICATION

It will be important for investigators to know basic terms used by dentists to describe teeth anatomy and shapes. This should allow them to understand dental reports and be able to discuss case specifics.

The two main sections of a tooth are: (1) the part that shows in the mouth (*crown*) and (2) the part embedded in the gums and jawbone (*root*). Some teeth have more than one root. The front teeth only have one root while the back teeth can have as many as four.

Each of the five surfaces of a crown have a specific name. The biting surface is called the *occlusal* for back teeth and *incisal* for the front teeth. The tooth surface touching the cheek and the surface towards the tongue are the *facial* and *lingual*, respectively. The side toward the front of the mouth is the *mesial* and the side toward the back is the *distal*. These words can also be used to describe tooth position. For example, a tooth may be tipped mesially (towards the front) or crowded in a lingual position (towards the tongue). Restorations (fillings and crowns) are described by the restorative material used and the surfaces involved. An individual silver filling that fills both the mesial and biting (occlusal) surfaces of a posterior tooth is called a *mesio-occlusal amalgam*. These definitions become crucial when charting the dental conditions present.

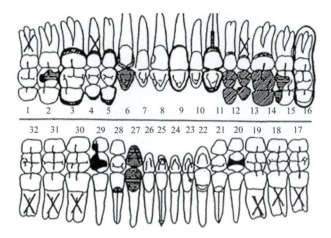

Figure 1.5

This is a dental chart showing all of the human adult teeth numbered in the Universal System that is popular in the US. The numerical sequence starts with the last upper adult tooth on the right side of the face (#1) and continues to #32. The symbols drawn on these teeth are diagrammatic descriptions of filling shape and location (as in #29), the presence of a crown covering a tooth (#27), or the tooth not being present in the mouth (#17, 18, and 19). The circle around #16 indicates the tooth is impacted (under the gum tissue). Teeth #3, 4, 5 show a fixed bridge. #4 was extracted (hence the "x" on its root) and teeth #3 and #5 were covered with crowns in order to connect a replacement tooth for #4.

It becomes obvious that the amount of potential information contained in a person's dental record can be enormous. The quality of an *antemortem* (before death) patient file will be directly related to the detail that the dentist included in his/her clinical examination and recorded on paper. The comparison for the purpose of dental identification becomes an impossible task without good records and exam radiographs.

The investigator should be aware of the general terms used by dentists and also be familiar with the shapes of different human teeth (Figure 1.5). This is to be aware of dental evidence and also to understand written dental records obtained in the course of a case. The next two sections include information that should provide basic information.

TOOTH NAMES AND QUANTITY OF TEETH IN ADULTS AND CHILDREN

These two tables describe the number of human teeth and their general shape.

Tooth type	Number of teeth	
	Upper jaw	Lower jaw
Deciduous (baby teeth)	10	10
Adult	16	16

Basic tooth shapes	Incisors	Canines	Bicuspids	Molars
General appearance	Front four teeth; all have thin edges; square shaped	"eyeteeth", cone-shaped	Two cusps	Square; 4 and 5 cusps; largest teeth in jaw

TOOTH TERMS USED TO DESCRIBE PARTS OF TEETH

Terms used to describe parts of teeth and jaws:

Crown	Clinical crown – portion of a tooth visible in the mouth.
Root	The portion of a tooth that normally is embedded in the jaw bone. In older persons, the root may also be exposed while in the mouth. After high-energy impacts, the entire tooth, both crown and root, may be fragmented away from the surrounding jaw.
CEJ	The *Cemento-Enamel Junction* – the neck of the tooth that demarcates the crown from the root.
Cusp	Biting edges of a tooth. Front teeth (the pairs of central, lateral, and cuspid incisors) in each jaw do not have cusps. The back teeth (bicuspids and molars) have flat biting surfaces that possess bumps called *cusps*.
Quadrant	Each jaw is divided into two halves which are labeled left and right. The entire human dentition (teeth) has four quadrants.
Incisors	The front four teeth in the upper (maxillary) and lower (mandibular) jaws.
Canine	Commonly known as the *eyetooth*, the canine has the longest root of any tooth. It is located next to the incisors and in front of the bicuspids.
Bicuspids	A set of two teeth behind each canine and in front of the molars. Generally, they have two roots. Also known as *premolars*.
Molars	The large, flat surfaced teeth that have multiple roots located in the back of the mouth.
Incisal	The biting edge of front teeth (incisors and canines).
Occlusal	The chewing surface of back teeth (premolars and molars).
Buccal	Tooth surfaces that touch the cheek. Term reserved for bicuspids and molars.
Labial	Tooth surface that touches the lips. Term reserved for front teeth (incisors). Also known as the *facial* surface.
Palatal	Upper bicuspid and molar surfaces facing the roof of the mouth (palate).
Lingual	Tooth surface that touches the tongue (front teeth).
Mesial	Tooth surface facing towards the midline of the face (line drawn from the nose to the chin).

Distal	Tooth surface facing away from the midline of the face.
Enamel	The hardest tissue in the human body that also covers the crowns of teeth.
Cementum	The root is made of this hard tissue which is much like bone.
Dentine	The softer material that is underneath the outer enamel layer.

HUMAN TOOTH MORPHOLOGY

Investigator and search team ability to identify and recover dental evidence is directly based on their education of what the various human teeth look like. Tooth morphology is the science of identifying different types of teeth.

FRONT TEETH

Human incisors have thin, knife-like crowns that are used for cutting and tearing food. There are two of this type in each jaw (the dental arch). The first incisor is called the *central incisor* and is located directly below the nose or above the chin (midline). The second incisor is the *lateral incisor* and its position is adjacent to the central incisor. The upper incisors and canines overlap (*overbite*) the lower teeth when the mouth is closed.

Maxillary central incisor

This is the most noticeable tooth in the mouth (Figure 1.6). It has a straight biting edge. Both sides are curved with the distal being more rounded. *Mammelons* are seen on the biting edges of newly erupted and unworn incisors of juveniles and young adults. These are bumps that wear down by the adult years. Mesial

Figure 1.6
Adult maxillary right central incisor.

and distal aspects present a distinctive triangular outline. This is true for all of the incisors.

An important shape variation of the upper incisors is the shovel shaped incisor. It presents as a large, scooped out indentation on the lingual (tongue side) surface. This feature is seen in populations having Mongolian racial origins.

Maxillary lateral incisor

The maxillary (upper) lateral incisor (Figure 1.7) resembles the central incisor but is narrower in width. The side surfaces have similar shapes as its two adjacent teeth, the central incisor and canine.

The tooth is narrow and can be peg-shaped (smaller and narrow). It is sometimes absent in 1–2% of the population. The back (lingual) surface can have deep pits often requiring fillings.

Canines

Canines (eyeteeth or cuspids) are the longest rooted teeth. This single-rooted tooth is present in each quadrant. The appearance of canines is a genetic trait seen in all *carnivores*. In color, this tooth appears darker (yellow or brown) than the adjacent teeth. This tooth functions with the incisors to tear and shred food. This may be the final tooth to be lost during life because it has a thick root, well embedded in bone. The mandibular canine is noticeably narrower in width than the upper and usually shorter (Figures 1.8 and 1.9).

Figure 1.7
Adult maxillary right lateral incisor.

Figure 1.8
Adult maxillary right canine.

Figure 1.9
Adult mandibular right canine.

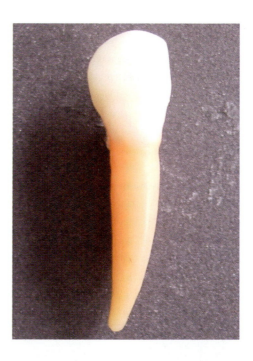

Mandibular central incisor

The mandibular (lower) central incisor (Figure 1.10) is the smallest tooth in the mouth. It is a long, narrow, symmetrical tooth. The biting edge is straight.

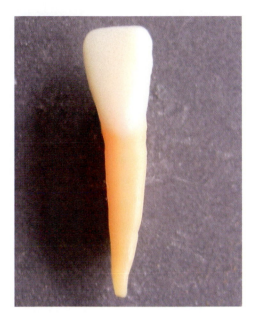

Figure 1.10
Adult mandibular right central incisor.

Mandibular lateral incisor

This tooth resembles the central incisor, but is a bit larger in most dimensions. The biting edge's shape assists in this tooth's identification. The edge is "bent" front to back, reflecting the curvature of the jaw (Figure 1.11).

BACK TEETH

Upper and lower bicuspids (premolars)

Bicuspids (two cusps) are located between the canine and molar teeth. There are two per quadrant and are identified as the first and second bicuspids. The upper have two well-defined cusps: buccal and lingual (Figures 1.12 and 1.13). The lower has one prominent cusp and another much smaller (Figures 1.14 and 1.15). The larger cusp is the buccal (towards the cheek).

MOLAR TEETH

Adult molars are located in the back of the jaw. They have the most chewing surface of any tooth and have three to five chewing cusps. Lower-jaw molars have two large roots and the upper-jaw molars have three roots.

Maxillary adult molar

The biting surface outline is square (not as much as the mandibular molars) with four distinct cusps. Some maxillary molars have an extra cusp (Carrabelli cusp)

Figure 1.11
Adult mandibular right lateral incisor.

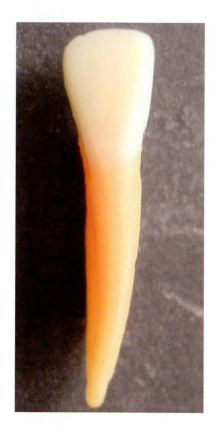

Figure 1.12
Adult maxillary right first premolar.

Figure 1.13
Adult maxillary right second premolar.

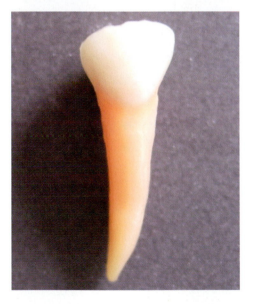

Figure 1.14
Adult mandibular right first premolar.

located on the mesiolingual cusp (tongue side of the tooth). There are three roots, two buccal and one lingual that is the longest of the three (Figures 1.16 and 1.17).

Maxillary third adult molar

They are the most often congenitally missing adult teeth. Third molars' shape is also the most variable of all human teeth and is the smallest of the maxillary molars. There are three roots: two buccal and one lingual that are generally fused together into an ice cream cone shape.

Figure 1.15
Adult mandibular right second premolar.

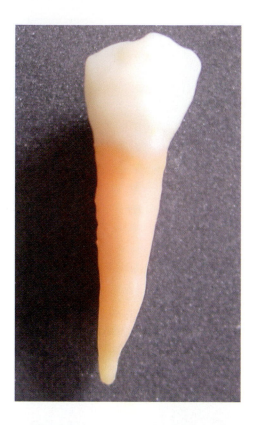

Figure 1.16
Adult maxillary right first molar.

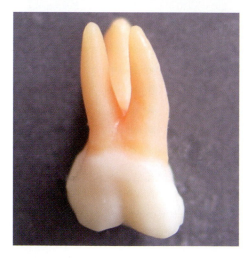

Mandibular first adult molar

The lower first adult molar (Figure 1.18) is the widest of all molar teeth and has two roots. This tooth possesses a five-sided (and five cusp) occlusal shape that is a classic feature.

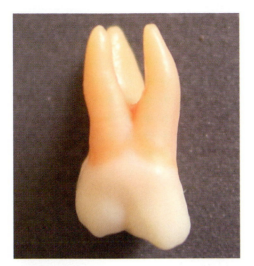

Figure 1.17
Adult maxillary right second molar.

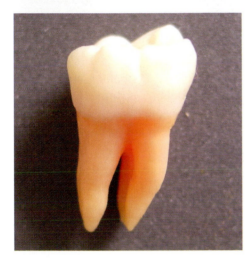

Figure 1.18
Adult mandibular right first molar.

Mandibular second molar

There are two roots that are shorter than the first molar (Figure 1.19).

Mandibular third molar

The two roots are short, curved and can be larger or smaller than the other molar teeth. The shapes of this tooth are variable with the tooth frequently not properly erupting into the oral cavity (impaction).

TOOTH NUMBERING SYSTEMS

Any investigator should have a basic understanding of how dentists number and describe features of specific teeth. The U.S. uses a number system called *Universal*

Figure 1.19
Adult mandibular right second molar.

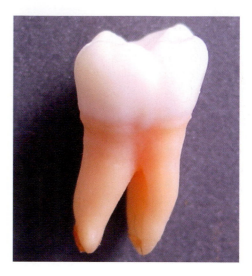

that labels adult teeth from 1 to 32. The baby teeth are labeled A through T. The first adult tooth numbered is always the upper right back tooth and is #1 and follows to the upper left back tooth called #16. The lower adult teeth start at #17 on the back lower left and continue to the right until #32 located at the back right of the dental arch. The baby teeth are arranged in the same manner, although an alphabetic system is used being A through J for the upper baby teeth and K through T for the lower baby teeth. The FDI (*Fédération Dentaire Internationale*) system predominates in Europe, Canada and British Commonwealth countries. The FDI uses a two number system where the first number is the quadrant (1 through 4) and the second number starts at 1 for the central incisor and continues toward the back teeth. Baby teeth have the numbers 5 through 8 to indicate the four possible quadrants (Figure 1.20). See Figure 1.20 for comparison of these two systems.

The upper jaw is called the *maxilla* and is solidly attached to the base of the skull. The lower jaw is the *mandible* and provides the movement when chewing and talking.

THE DENTAL INVESTIGATOR'S ROLE IN FORENSIC CASE WORK

Forensic dentists address diverse medico-legal issues that can aid agencies and individuals who have questions relating to dentistry. The author has been contacted by local police agencies, the State Attorney General, Medical Examiners, criminal defense attorneys, private parties, State courts, the Department of Justice and the National Institute of Justice for dental opinions. The contact usually begins with a phone call.

The identification of missing and unknown persons is a central activity that predominates in a forensic dentistry practice. It is highly advantageous for the

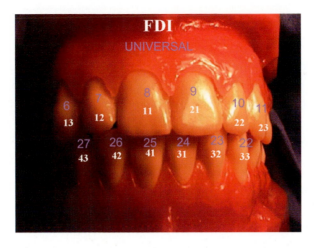

Figure 1.20

The Universal System (in blue) contrasted with the FDI System (in white) for the twelve adult front teeth.

Adult teeth

Upper right   Upper left

Universal	1	2	3	4	5	6	7	8	9	10	11	12	13	14	15	16
FDI	18	17	16	15	14	13	12	11	21	22	23	24	25	26	27	28

Lower right   Lower left

Universal	32	31	30	29	28	27	26	25	24	23	22	21	20	19	18	17
FDI	48	47	46	45	44	43	42	41	31	32	33	34	35	36	37	38

Deciduous (Baby teeth)

Upper right   Upper left

Universal	A	B	C	D	E	F	G	H	I	J
FDI	55	54	53	52	51	61	62	63	64	65

Lower right   Lower left

Universal	T	S	R	Q	P	O	N	M	L	K
FDI	85	84	83	82	81	71	72	73	74	75

dentist to attend the autopsy. Some cases, however, have the initial contact much later in an investigation.

A dental identification of an unknown person can involve participation in autopsy examinations at the request of law enforcement, Coroners or Medical Examiners at local or state level. This postmortem-dental examination of human remains involves charting dental and cranial features, radiographic documentation of these features and forensic report writing regarding these findings. A second step is the application of these findings to investigations by law enforcement to identify a missing or an unknown person. The physical comparison of autopsy results and antemortem dental radiographs and records completes the process wherein the dentist renders an opinion of either a positive identification, a possible identification, no identification or inconclusive results.

COLLECTING AND PRESERVING USEFUL EVIDENCE

Law enforcement plays a pivotal role because of their early presence at a crime scene, accident or involvement in death investigation. This book's intention is to give the officer or technician arriving at a scene or an autopsy, sufficient information to identify and collect dental evidence that comes across their paths.

CASE TYPES THAT CAN POSSESS DENTAL EVIDENCE

1. Homicide
   - Sexual assault with bite marks.
   - Unknown victim of a crime found in a skeletonized or decomposed condition.
   - A deceased attacker may have bite mark injuries that can be used to corroborate the victim's statement.
   - A deceased child may have bite mark injuries that indicate current or past physical abuse. The identity of the biter may be supported by a dentist and by obtaining swabbings of the injuries for DNA analysis of deposited saliva.
2. Child abuse.
3. Spousal abuse.
4. Elder abuse.
5. Mass disaster.
6. Age determination of a juvenile offender.

WHO QUALIFIES AS A DENTAL EXPERT?

The courtroom use of an experienced forensic dentist is recommended for obvious reasons. In the U.S. and elsewhere, the use of a dentist with no forensic training and experience is generally acceptable but will raise the issues of the *value* or *legal weight* given to opinions given in the court. The expert must be someone who understands the significance of the relationship of law and dentistry and can explain the complexities and subtleties of dental evidence to the courts. Technical expertise in forensic odontology is not based on the current curriculum available in traditional dental education. In a practical sense, the U.S. courts accept testimony from anyone who will aid the court in areas beyond the knowledge of lay people. The court considers the combination of education, training and experience and the relationship to the case currently at trial when permitting a dentist to testify.

   The forensic odontologist not only has to be an experienced practitioner of clinical dentistry but someone who is also able to observe, record, gather, preserve and interpret dental evidence. The next task requires concise and balanced communication to law enforcement, prosecution and defense counsel, the court and the jury.

COURTROOM USES OF DENTAL EVIDENCE

The admission of expert testimony derived from dental evidence is a compelling factor in criminal cases where assault, abuse, homicide and physical evidence reveal tooth marks in skin and objects or genomic DNA obtained from trace saliva samples, tooth pulp and roots. The historical uses of tooth mark impressions (*bite mark analysis*) and *dental identification* have recently been augmented with *bio-molecular* techniques (DNA) used in other areas of human biology. The early role of a relatively small number of dentists in court proceedings has progressed substantially over the past 25 years due. This is due in part to the general acceptance of the forensic odontological community that questions of reliability of methods and opinions are satisfied by the years of experience, credentials, some empirical testing and considerable anecdotal reporting. An additional assurance, using a mode of circular logic, is the fact that the judiciary has admitted bite mark analysis in every state. There is little doubt in judicial case law that dentists play a role in determining questions of fact relevant to criminal and civil proceedings.

CHILD, SPOUSAL AND ELDER ABUSE

In the last three decades, the unfortunate prevalence of violence perpetrated against domestic partners, children and the elderly has necessitated the involvement of the forensic dentist in its recognition and documentation. In most states, all custodial adults' medical and dental professionals are mandated reporters in the suspicion of child abuse. A patient may visit the general practice with dental injuries that are not consistent with the clinical findings. The parent or guardian may avoid discussion about the events surrounding the injury or the injury may be one in a series of "accidents". Head, neck trauma and oral and facial injuries are common to child abuse situations. Severe or repeated incidents are suggestive of abuse.

JURISPRUDENCE

Another area of activity is expert testimony in civil litigation involving dental issues such as personal injury law, workers compensation, professional malpractice and disputes regarding aspects of the dentist-patient relationship. Injuries to the oral structures may result from auto accidents, falls on private or commercial property or an accident in the workplace. Litigation may follow. Both sides require the interpretation of an expert who is familiar with the legal and clinical terminology related to diagnosis, treatment planning, procedure and sequelae (post operative complications).

EMPLOYMENT

Experienced forensic odontologists generally have formal appointments or consulting relationships with Coroners, Medical Examiners, state and local government agencies and branches of the military. Reimbursement is on a fee-for-service or contractual basis.

SCIENTIFIC DENTAL INVESTIGATIONS

The subject matter of forensic dental investigations can be as simple as being asked to compare two sets of dental radiographs for common features. Alternatively, a series of scientific studies may be needed to be conducted relating to specific questions pertaining to a case. In this instance, it is mandatory that the odontologist involved uses methods that have been reliably tested and that others can reproduce. This form of *ad hoc* experimentation is affected in that the experimenter already knows the facts of the case and is generally employed by only one of the involved parties. The basis of an expert dentist's opinion should not involve personal opinion, assumptions of untested hypotheses and over statements of the value of the original evidence.

THE MOST FAMOUS BITEMARK CASE OF THE 20TH CENTURY

A particularly well-known bite mark case in the U.S. is the dental evidence brought against executed serial murderer Theodore (Ted) Bundy (Figure 1.21) in a Florida court. The case involved a double murder and aggravated assault that occurred in 1978. The dental evidence centered on a skin injury on the

Figure 1.21

Ted Bundy is suspected of having abducted and murdered over 30 women over a 10-year period.

body of one of the murder victims. The prosecution dental experts considered these marks to have been made by human teeth. Defense experts considered the bite mark evidence to be non-specific for Bundy's teeth (Figures 1.22–1.24). Other physical evidence obtained from Bundy and later associated to the crime included hair samples from one victim's bedroom. The jury, in reviewing the evidence, convicted Bundy of murder. They attested that the bite mark evidence was very compelling. This case occurred before the advent of DNA analysis from saliva taken from bite mark injuries.

DENTAL IDENTIFICATION OF ADOLF HITLER

The disappearance and death of Adolf Hitler in April 1945 remained a long unanswered puzzle until 1968 when the Russian writer Lev Brezhymenski published a book entitled "The Death of Adolf Hitler". He noted documents from Soviet archives that supported identification procedures on the human

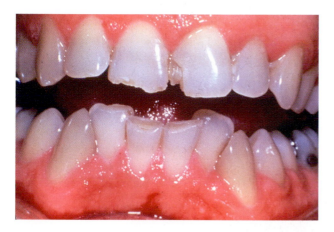

Figure 1.22

An intra-oral photograph of Ted Bundy. The lower front teeth proved to be useful at trial to link him to a bite mark found on a murdered college student.

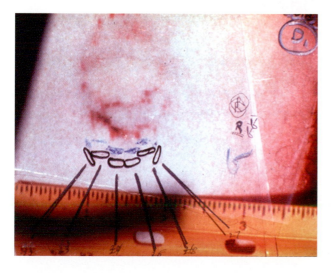

Figure 1.23

Courtroom exhibit showing the injury pattern is actually two bite marks nearly superimposed in the same area. The wooden ruler was used to allow the picture to be enlarged to life-size. Two hand-drawn outlines of Bundy's lower teeth are placed just below a corresponding portion of the bite mark.

Figure 1.24

Close-up view of the bite marks with the outline of the lower teeth digitally superimposed on the lower most injury pattern. The arrangement of five Bundy's lower six teeth coincide with the reddened bruises.

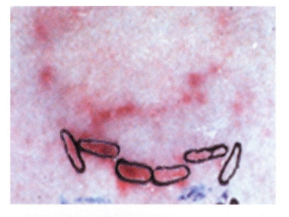

Figure 1.25

The Fuhrer in 1934. This shows Hitler's lower front teeth (white circle). A digital enlargement of these teeth was used to compare with the dental remains the Russians recovered in 1945 from outside his Berlin bunker.

remains performed by the Russians after their capture of Berlin at the end of World War II. The book included descriptive information of Hitler's alleged corpse with photographs of remaining postmortem dental restorations and some of his natural teeth still in the mandible. Figures 1.25 and 1.26 show a digital analysis of Hitler's teeth before and after death. The amount of evidence available is not ideal, but the outcome is compelling.

Hitler's dental remains

Maxilla　What remained of the upper jaw was a nine-tooth fixed bridge with four natural teeth remaining. The bridge contained a series of replacement teeth that were attached to teeth at both ends.

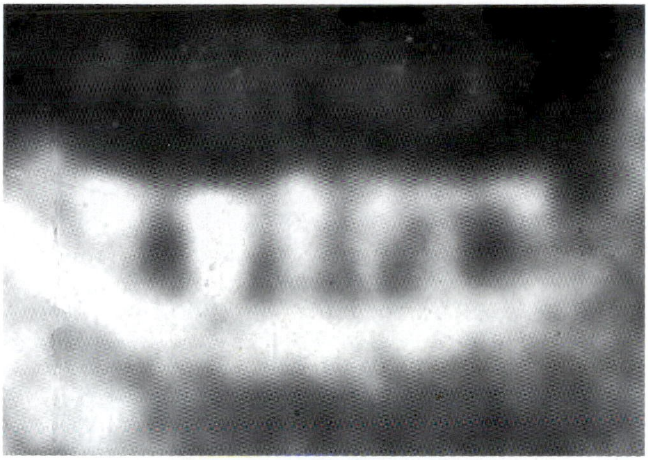

Figure 1.26

Close-up of the teeth circled in Figure 1.25. The fuzziness can be partially resolved via the use of Adobe Photoshop® and then placed over photographs of the remains obtained in 1945.

Mandible Five untreated natural anterior teeth were present in the mandible and showed advanced gum disease as well as signs of erosion and abrasion. On the left, three abutments supported a six-tooth bridge while two natural teeth on the right side supported a four-teeth bridge with a replacement tooth in the back.

No X-rays were included with the Russian documents but a record of the interrogation of Hitler's dentist found among documents in American archives provided a description of his dental history and status with diagrammatic information.

After an assassination attempt on July 20, 1944, five X-rays of Hitler's head were made for diagnostic purposes. These were later located in the U.S. National Archives and they permitted several important diagnostic observations as a contribution to an identification (Figure 1.27).

Examination of these cranial radiographic plates showed that most of the large posterior teeth on the right side of both jaws were missing and suggested the presence of teeth back to the third molar area on the lower left side. The anterior portion of the maxillary teeth showed extensive metal restorations. These findings, among others, were consistent with previous odontological observations. The presence of bone resorption (bone loss) in the lower jaw was also confirmed in the front-view of the mandible.

In the preparation of this analysis, almost all of the stills or static photographs of Hitler examined provided no relevant information as they did not show any "toothy" features. However, a search in the archives of the National Swiss Film Museum (Cinématheque Suisse, Lausanne) provided documents where Hitler was showing his teeth while giving a speech or smiling. These documents covered a period between 1934 and 1944 when, according to statements made by the dentist who treated him during that time, Hitler underwent no further major dental treatment other than that present at the time of his death. The stills were selected

Figure 1.27

The head X-ray of Adolf Hitler taken in 1944.

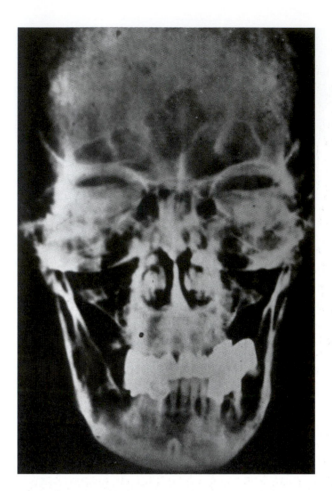

Figure 1.28

Photograph of the lower jaw recovered in 1945 by Russians who captured the Fuhrer's bunker. The circled teeth will be superimposed onto the head X-ray of Hitler (Figure 1.29).

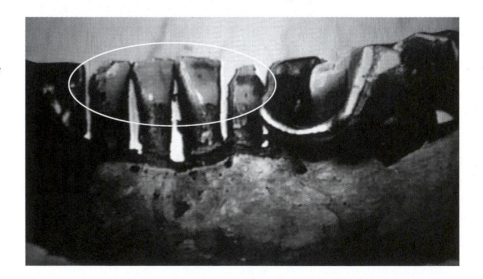

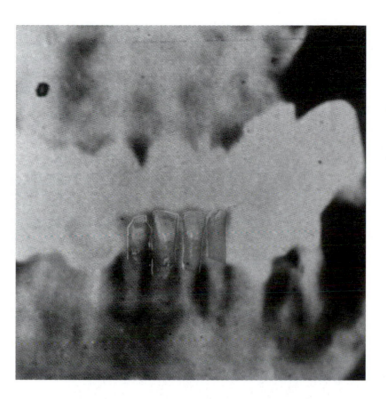

Figure 1.29

Overlaying the four postmortem teeth onto the head X-ray shows similarity of root width and tooth position. This digital analysis shows consistency between the jaw recovered in 1945 and the X-ray dated 1944. This dental identification should not be considered conclusive.

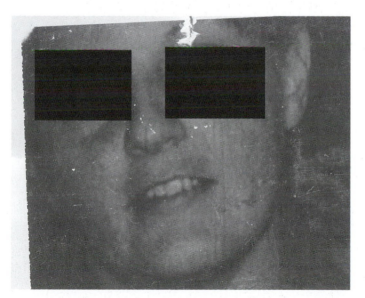

Figure 1.30

The missing person's report included a photograph of the young woman. The investigator thought the woman's front teeth "looked odd". There were no formal dental records available for this woman as she rarely had dental care.

from German newsreels, motion pictures on Hitler's life and Leni Riefenstahl's propaganda films "Triumph of the Will" and "Olympic Games 1936". Figure 1.28 shows human remains found in 1945 in Berlin and represented by the Soviet Union as being Adolf Hitler. Also see Figure 1.29.

WOMAN'S IDENTITY CONFIRMED BY A MISSING TOOTH

A skeletonized female body was found in a ravine behind of biker bar in California. The remains had few personal effects but police had a missing person's report that provided a lead. Figures 1.30–1.32 show the dental evidence available in this case.

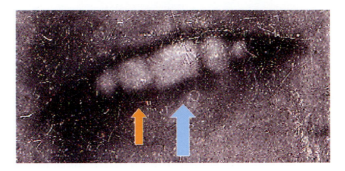

Figure 1.31

The forensic dentist confirmed that the woman was missing an upper central incisor (front tooth #8) sometime in the past, as there was no residual space or gap. The adjacent teeth had moved together to give a relatively normal appearance. The orange arrow points to tooth #7, and the blue arrow points to tooth #9.

Figure 1.32

Digital enhancement of original autopsy image. The skeletonized head shows two front teeth missing after death (open sockets of #9 and #10) but no socket for the long-time missing front tooth (#8). The dental evidence confirmed the dental profile of the missing woman. It is unlikely that the body is someone else due to all the circumstances and supporting evidence comparisons.

CHAPTER 2

THE EVIDENCE, THE FORENSIC DENTIST AND DENTAL ANALYSIS

CASE STUDIES OF DEATH AND ABUSE INVESTIGATIONS

A patrol car with two county sheriff officers are sent on a tip to investigate a report from a confidential informant that a missing adult female had been murdered and dumped in a ravine outside the city limits. The officers arrived on the scene and observed a blue 55-gallon plastic drum resting in the bottom of a deep ditch adjacent to a country road. Search and Rescue retrieved the container. The contents were a combination of concrete rubble and human remains. The body was in an advanced state of decomposition. Clothing found in the vicinity was attributed to the missing woman. Law enforcement needed a positive confirmation of the identity and the cause of death. The manner of death as homicide was obvious from the circumstances. The container with its contents was transported to the county medical examiner's office where the pathologist and the staff removed the body from the encasing concrete. No documentation or identity papers were on the body. The body was too decomposed for fingerprints to be taken. Visual identification was impossible although the remains were female and the general age of the missing woman could be estimated. No tattoos, scars or medical implants presented which could be used to affirm a likely identity. The forensic dentist arrived to assist in removing the jaws (acceptable in a non-viewable case) and provide a complete dental exam with X-rays. The original missing persons report included two dental X-rays taken 9 years previously when the woman was 10 years old. The dental history (taken from written notes of the treating dentist) indicated a silver-amalgam filling placed on the upper right first permanent molar 10 years previous. One old X-ray showed the presence of this filling. The autopsy dental X-ray showed a filling present in the same tooth. No other teeth had been filled, extracted, capped or otherwise altered by dental treatment. Once the autopsy dental exam was finished, the forensic dentist used a computer program to digitally compare these

Figure 2.1

This adult male was recovered on an ocean beach after being reported missing for over a week. The cause of death was drowning and the manner of death was accidental. The condition of the facial tissues prevents visual identification as a reliable means of identity determination. Dental records (written and X-rays) were obtained by law enforcement and used to compare with dental findings obtained at autopsy. The few teeth remaining in the jaws were consistent with the dental records and the identification was determined by the medical examiner.

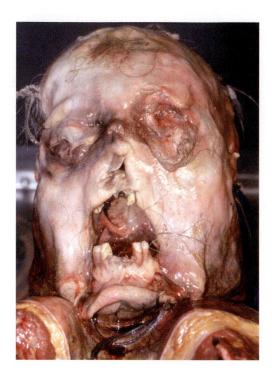

sets of X-rays and he stated that the outline, shape and position of the single filling is sufficient to identify the body as that of the missing woman. A DNA analysis of the unidentified body's genetic code and the genetic profile of the missing girl's family could have accomplished the same result at a much higher cost and considerably longer processing time.

DENTAL RECORDS ARE IMPORTANT INVESTIGATIVE TOOLS

The usefulness of dental identifications is well documented in the professional forensic journals and the popular media. In death investigation, the cases of drowning or water immersion for prolonged lengths of time pose a problem in getting a timely identification. Bodies severely decomposed and swollen from water absorption will lack clothing holding identification papers. Tattoos and jewelry may or may not be present. DNA may be possible, but can take weeks to months for results. The case (Figure 2.1) is a good example of these circumstances.

MEDICAL RECORDS ARE IMPORTANT INVESTIGATIVE TOOLS

Missing person files must include the individual's medical history and dental history. This information, if available, is a vital potential link between any

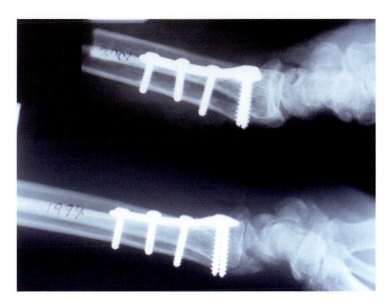

Figure 2.2

Police investigators obtained medical records created in 1994 for a person reported missing for 2 weeks. The records indicated the person had been treated for a fractured forearm. At the time a stainless steel fixation device was placed with screws and remained in place. The autopsy X-rays determined the presence of a similar device in the same forearm of found human remains. The concordance of shape and materials of this device is seen in both the antemortem (bottom) and postmortem radiographs (the X-ray on top was taken during autopsy in 2001).

recovered human remains and a possible identity. Investigators should be determined to follow leads towards any source of medical information. The following case is a good example of how one good medical X-ray can lead to identification[1] (Figure 2.2). See Chapter 7 for the complete case analysis.

[1] Bowers CM, Johansen RJ. Digital imaging methods as an aid in dental identification of human remains. *J Forensic Sci* 2002; 47(2): 354–359. Reprint permission granted by ASTM, Inc.

CASE TYPES

A forensically-trained and court-experienced dentist can be asked to consult on cases by a wide variety of government agencies and individuals (Table 2.1).

CASE STUDY OF POSSIBLE CHILD ABUSE

The CPS investigator called a forensic dentist to enquire about the chances to look at some polaroid pictures of a child recently placed in foster care. The dentist arrived at the CPS office and was given three photographs showing a 9-year old child with various "cuts and tears" around his mouth. The dentist suggested a visit with the child to do a dental examination. The child was seen and the dentist determined that the child has not been the victim of physical child

Table 2.1

Agency	Case type
Child Protective Services (CPS)	Child abuse
Senior Support Agency	Elder abuse or neglect
Coroner	Unidentified human remains, Bite mark on deceased person
District attorney	Homicide or assault
Defense counsel	Homicide or assault
Juvenile court	Age estimation (minor or adult age)
Hospital emergency room	Dental injury assessment; Bite mark evidence on live assault victim
Crime lab	Bite mark on food or gum obtained from a crime scene
State emergency services	Mass disaster identification of victims from airline accidents, floods, earthquakes and terrorist acts
Human rights organizations	Identify victims of genocide and politically motivated homicide
Anthropologists	Determination of identity via dental work and cranial anatomy
Religious organizations	Verification of remains purported to be human or non-human (e.g. Buddha's tooth or extraterrestrial remains?)
Legal organizations	Post-trial and appellate attorney's involved in review of death penalty convictions based, in whole or in part, on dental evidence
Family members	Survivors want an independent review of identifications done by law enforcement or coroner's agencies

abuse, but rather, from a systemic (medical) disorder that caused severe skin scabbing and oral lesions.

CASE STUDY OF A CHILD'S DEATH BY CANINE ATTACK

Investigators must be aware of the types of injuries seen in sharp force trauma cases. The ability to differentiate between knife wounds, bite marks, insect bites, abrasions and other mechanisms that injure skin is vital. Also, the investigator must know when the findings are vague, or confused and not specific for just one cause. Knife and teeth wounds can be amazingly similar. One may be an accident but the other is certainly a homicide (Figures 2.3 and 2.4).

THE PRIMARY ROLE OF THE FORENSIC ODONTOLOGIST IS HUMAN IDENTIFICATION

Forensic dentists address diverse medico-legal issues relating to the question "who is this person?". The identification of missing and unknown persons is the dentist's central activity and is extremely useful when photographs, fingerprints and DNA profiling are not possible or practical. Dentists participate in autopsy examinations at the request of law enforcement, coroners or medical examiners

Figure 2.3

The death of an infant for any reason is tragic. This young child died from sharp force injuries. The perpetrator was a dog. The deep incisions in the neck mimic knife wounds. It is important to understand the subtle markings in these injuries and the overall circumstances of a case that indicate an animal versus a human attacker. The dog's canine teeth created these injuries. The child's skin and clothing can be analyzed for animal DNA to confirm the contact between the victim and the dog.

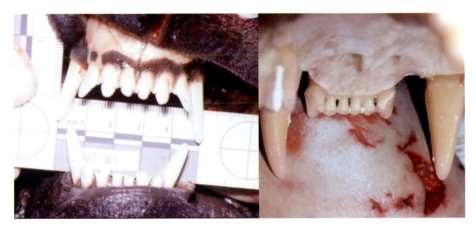

Figure 2.4

The left image is of an adult dog, which proves how effective the front teeth are for tearing and ripping. In the author's experience, the single dog will choose a prey that commonly is a child. Packs of dogs easily can attack an adult human. The distance between the large canine teeth in this animal is 5 cm. The number of incisors between these canines totals six, versus only four for humans. The right image shows the upper jaw of a California cougar superimposed on its victim's shaven skull. The crescent-shaped puncture wound in this picture can be mistaken for knife or human bite marks. The animal's DNA will be present on the victim's skin and clothing and should be analyzed to identify the attacker.

at the local or state level. The postmortem dental examination of human remains involves charting dental and cranial features, radiographic documentation of these features and forensic report writing regarding these findings. A second step is the application of these findings to investigations by law enforcement that attempt to develop leads and record documentation to identify a missing or unknown person. The physical comparison of autopsy results and antemortem dental radiographs and records completes the process wherein the dentist renders either an opinion of a positive identification, a possible identification, no identification or inconclusive results (Figure 2.5).

VIABILITY: TEETH ARE NEARLY INDESTRUCTIBLE

The viability of teeth and jaws remaining intact in the aftermath of extreme temperatures, explosions and other disintegrating events where people die is the central reason for forensic dentistry's role in medico-legal death investigation. Teeth are constructed of dense and hard materials called *enamel* and *dentin* that resist total destruction or decay, even when burned, fragmented or buried in the ground. In all these circumstances, teeth often outlast bone.

Situations that may make dental identifications necessary on a large scale include mass disasters, transportation accidents, acts of war/aggression and

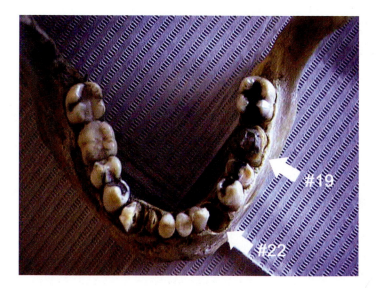

Figure 2.5

This dried mandible was recovered from a desert area of California. There is no soft tissue left attached to the bone, which reduces the smell to minimal odor. The lower left first molar (see arrow #19) shows the appearance of having once been covered by a crown. The tooth has been reshaped for a "full" crown. Tooth #22 shows an open socket that indicates the tooth was present during life. A healed socket (the bone has filled in the socket) indicates the tooth being pulled before death.

terrorism. Mass disasters may result from the forces of nature, like earthquakes, tornados, hurricanes, floods, fires and typhoons. Transportation accidents include air, marine, rail and surface vehicular transit modes. Acts of war, aggression and terrorism may create victim identification requiring the assistance of the forensic dental specialist.

Case study

Police and fire units had arrived due to a fire call in the early morning. Human remains were found in a dumpster behind a convenience store. Fire personnel removed the remains from the dumpster and the Coroner Service transported them to the morgue. The body was severely burned which was notable by its charred torso and head with a total loss of arms and legs. Experts considered the fire to have reached over 1,000°C and was enhanced by use of an accelerant. Dissection of the jaws from the charred face and skull revealed severely burned front teeth. There were no dental restorations present in the mouth. The recent report of a missing adult female then led investigators to consider a possible identity. Their lead was confirmed from the woman's family, as DNA analysis was successfully performed on an impacted (still enclosed in bone) third molar (wisdom tooth). This tooth was chosen due to its relative protection from the intense heat of the fire (Figure 2.6). Extreme temperatures will destroy the DNA found in erupted teeth.

Criminal and death investigation cases utilize the services of a forensic odontologist. They include industrial or domestic explosions where fragmentation

Figure 2.6

This one tooth may be all that is left of the deceased individual. The tooth is nearly incinerated to ash by a high temperature fire. This results in the tooth being extremely fragile and possibly smaller in size due to heat-caused shrinkage. The tooth should be removed (placed in a Tupperware cup and padded with Kleenex) from the scene only after it has been stabilized with a coating of hair spray or clear artist's lacquer. In this case, heat from the fire renders DNA analysis impossible when a tooth is exposed directly to high temperatures. The dental characteristics of the tooth, however, may produce identification from old dental X-rays and records. Photograph the tooth in position before attempting to remove it. The scale helps in re-creating a life-size picture.

makes identification a challenge. Accidental or suicidal drowning, where bloat-ing, decomposition and marine life activity, make visual identification impos-sible. Discovered human remains can be recovered from construction sites, crime scenes, storage spaces, dump sites and motor vehicle accidents. The link-ing of missing persons reports with Jane or John Doe unidentified bodies is a task that permits closure for those families. At the same time, law enforcement is provided with important identification information on victims of violent crime (Figure 2.7).

THE NECESSITY FOR POSITIVE HUMAN IDENTIFICATION

The effects of positively identifying individuals have considerable humanitarian value for families and society. Making a positive identification of an unidentified

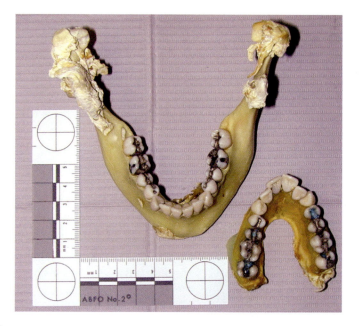

Figure 2.7

At autopsy, these human jaws were dissected from a badly decomposed body in order to aid the examination. The lower jaw (mandible: center of picture) has been removed from the skull by cutting it away from the supporting muscles. The upper jaw (at the lower right) was removed from the front of the skull with a Stryker bone saw. It is important to make the cut high above the ends of the upper teeth to avoid destroying tooth roots that can be useful for identification because of their shape. The specialized ruler is an ABFO No. 2 scale developed by Dr. Tom Krauss and William Hyzer. It is used extensively in bite mark analysis (see the accompanying chapter on digital analysis techniques). A body that is amenable to a visual identification and may be viewable by family should never have the jaws removed in this manner. Rigor mortis (postmortem stiffening) may prevent opening the deceased's jaw for a period of time, but will dissipate in a day or so after death.

body is crucial to many police and legal matters. It permits the issuance of a death certificate that is necessary for the settlement of estate, probate and insurance policies. Additionally, resolution of child custody, property issues and remarriage of the surviving spouse are made possible. Of equal importance is the release of the identified remains to the family for burial and final disposition. Without positive identification a family can spend a lifetime wondering if their loved one was in fact a victim. Fruitless searching and hoping may be the alternative to knowing the fate of their loved one.

In a death investigation where there is evidence indicating that death occurred at the hands of another, a positive identification allows law enforcement to proceed with investigation and potential prosecution.

HOW DENTAL IDENTIFICATION IS POSSIBLE

The average human through the periods of development from child to adulthood possesses, at different stages, 20 baby teeth and 32 adult teeth. Some of this total of 52 teeth may be present in a 2-year-old infant or a 90-year-old person.

The adult human dentition consists of 16 teeth in the upper (maxilla) and 16 teeth in the lower (mandible) jaw. Occasionally, there will be extra teeth (supernumerary) present that may be useful in identifying an unknown person. There are four incisors, two cuspids (canine teeth), four premolars (bicuspids) and six molars in each jaw. Each adult jaw contains four anterior incisors, followed by one cuspid and two premolars on each side. The last three teeth in the posterior are the molars. Any of these teeth may be present in the mouth, present in the jaw but un-erupted into the oral cavity or congenitally absent. Teeth may be missing due to professional extraction or traumatically avulsed due to mishap or violence. A recently removed tooth leaves an extraction site in the jawbone which may be in various stages of healing at the time of death. That process can be used to estimate the time since tooth loss. Teeth lost due to assault or postmortem decomposition are detectable through the absence of healing present in the residual jawbone.

Children possess 20 deciduous teeth which erupt during the first two years of life. They fall out (exfoliate) in a sequence and rate that is chronologically variable between different children. Dental data exists for the timing of these events in the general human population. The deciduous dentition contains only 10 teeth in each arch. There are only four small baby molars (in each jaw) and no premolars at all. Children will frequently display a mixed dentition that possesses some deciduous teeth and some permanent teeth. This begins to happen about 6 years of age and ceases when adult teeth replace the deciduous teeth about the age of 12 years. The presence or absence of certain teeth is a fundamental guideline for age determination. This can be of importance in incidents where there are several juveniles involved of similar age. Dental maturity generally occurs at the age of 18–20 years when the final set of molars (wisdom teeth or third molars) complete their development. Some people, however, do not possess these teeth.

THE RADIOGRAPHIC APPEARANCE OF BABY (DECIDUOUS) TEETH

The baby teeth shown in Figures 2.8 and 2.9 have the Universal System coding system labels. Baby teeth are much different from that of adult teeth. They most often have the permanent teeth showing underneath awaiting later eruption.

INVESTIGATIVE CLUES: JAW AND BONE STRUCTURE OF THE HEAD

Beyond looking at teeth, the forensic odontologist has training to investigate the other structures of the head and neck. Certainly, this is an area of overlap

Figure 2.8

These are the upper front four baby teeth (D, E, F, G) that are called incisors. The adult teeth numbered 7, 8, 9 and 10 (Universal system) will absorb the roots of the baby teeth and erupt into the mouth between the ages of 6–8 years old. This individual was about 3½ years old at the time of death.

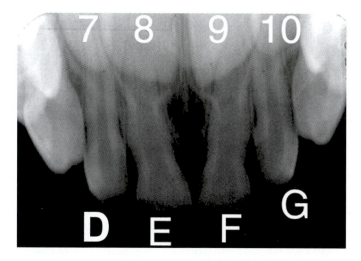

Figure 2.9

The lower left baby molar is "K." The permanent molars are either still under the gum tissue (19) or still encased in the jaw bone (18).

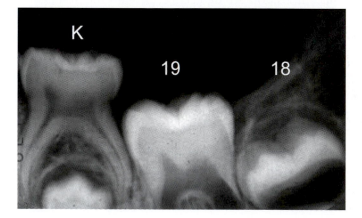

amongst dentist, pathologist and anthropologist. The final determination of a body's identity, age, sex and cause of death may be a collaborative effort of all three (or more) specialties. The important dental structures besides teeth are the bony prominences that may be present in either jaw and may be associated with old medical or dental records. These bumps or ridges may be on the palate (roof of the mouth) or on the external surfaces of the maxilla or on the internal or external surfaces of the mandible. They are relatively common and do not represent disease. Another variable may be the presence of melanin pigmentation on the soft tissue of the gingiva (gums). This feature may be visible in a nearly decomposed body and may indicate possible racial characteristics of the victim.

A recovered skull may contain evidence of trauma that occurred antemortem or postmortem. The antemortem changes may be used to make a possible identification. The skull may show these injuries as old fractures. These healed areas of injury show as ridges or areas of deformity that show up on X-ray. Facial injuries include trauma such as a fractured nose, cheekbone, jaw, and actual skull fracture. Injuries in children usually heal and the bone reconstructs itself back to normal shape over time. However, recent fractures up to a year may still be visible. Multiple fractures of facial or long bones in children have to be considered either abuse or a sign of congenital disease (osteogenesis imperfecta).

If bone fractures are treated, often there are metal devices implanted in the bone to aid in stabilizing the break. These devices easily show up on X-ray and can range from screws, pins, plates and rods. The actual device may be recovered at autopsy to investigate the presence of manufacturer identifiers such as part and lot number.

Analysis of the bone shapes seen in autopsy X-rays and old medical X-rays can lead to identifications (Figures 2.10 and 2.11).

VARIATION OF TOOTH SHAPE AND OTHER FEATURES

The teeth that are present in the mouth may be in perfect orthodontic alignment, widely spaced, tipped in a forward or backward dimension, rotated or crowded. Their biting surfaces may all be on a similar plane or some teeth may be higher or lower. The teeth may be decayed or filled with various materials. There are varieties of materials, either metallic, porcelain or plastic that are used to fill and restore the teeth. There may be individual crowns (caps) present or bridgework that spans several teeth and creates replacements between the anchor teeth. There may be chips, fractures or wear facets (worn spots) present near the chewing surfaces. There may be evidence of erosion or abrasion of the root surfaces at the gum line. In addition, there may be intrinsic

Figure 2.10

This is head X-ray of a deceased male. These skeletonized human remains were recovered without any personal identification. Police had a possible identification. Confirmation via dental means was impossible due to no availability of antemortem dental records. There was a history of a head X-ray taken at a local hospital belonging to the missing male. This was obtained (Figure 2.11) and compared to the X-ray of the deceased male. The area outlined in white is called the frontal sinus and is considered an individualizing feature (each person's frontal sinus is different).

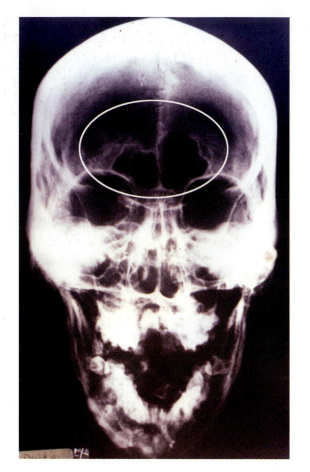

staining, developmental hypocalcification (compromised enamel) or other congenital anomalies that may distinguish a particular tooth or teeth. Poor oral hygiene combined with orthodontic bands can also produce a distinctive appearance.

The aforementioned characteristics of the teeth are visible upon clinical examination of the mouth. Radiographs will reveal many more important features that will serve to make a positive identification much more convincing. The radiographic examination may show the presence of un-erupted teeth, especially though not exclusively, third molars. The shape and depth of existing restorations can be seen. In the case of composite (combination of plastic and/or glass) materials, which are tooth colored, a restoration may only be clearly seen in a radiograph (X-ray) (Figure 2.12). The roots of teeth may yield a wealth of information. Tooth length, width, degree of enamel calcification in a young person, shape and angulations are all possible unique characteristics. The presence of endodontic treatment (root canal therapy) as well as the material used to complete the procedure (usually a crown or a filling) will be visible in a radiograph.

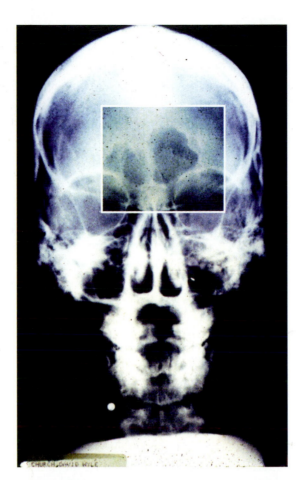

Figure 2.11
This is the older head X-ray that is digitally enhanced to reveal the shape of the sinus area. The sinus outlines in both the X-rays (Figures 2.10 and 2.11) are the same and the dead body and the known subject are identical.

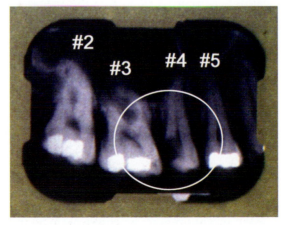

Figure 2.12
This is a dental X-ray obtained during autopsy. The circled area shows a large area of decay on tooth #4 (upper right second bicuspid). The roots of the two molars (#2 and #3) are curved. The white areas are metal fillings. The molars each have two fillings. The first bicuspid (#5) has one.

The radiographs will also show the supporting structure of the teeth. The trabecular (honey-comb appearance) pattern of the bone, the presence of tumors, cysts, any infectious process (abcess, cyst or tumor) or fracture and the shape of the sinus cavities can be important identifiers. Prosthetic dental implants may be present in the bone allowing for the fabrication of sophisticated prosthetic tooth replacements. Type, material, shape and size give implants quite a range of diversity and possess potential for important comparisons in a dental identification case. Composition of dental materials may be identified via sophisticated laboratory analyses (e.g., SEM-EDX). This may create a narrowing of possible sources of the material to a particular dental office or national origin.

INVESTIGATIVE STEPS IN DENTAL IDENTIFICATION

AT THE CRIME SCENE

The presence of a deceased person at a crime scene may be either patently obvious or come as a surprise sometime during the scene search. In the latter situation, what is done or not done before this discovery can later be a challenge at trial. The delayed determination that a burglary scene is actually a homicide scene can set any supervising detective's stomach churning. The adherence to set protocols and being observant without assuming only the obvious, once processing a scene commences, can alleviate the change of direction that may occur as time goes on.

PRELIMINARY EXAMINATION OF THE SCENE

As described earlier, the crime scene is subject to sudden changes and should be considered an evolving or dynamic event during processing. There is also a potential for a scene to be revisited much later with completely different investigative perspective. Contrasting this scenario with the fact that most evidence does not last forever makes the initial working of a crime scene very important. Evidence becomes of lesser and lesser value as time goes on. Dental evidence may be hidden in burned out rubble from an arson fire and will be lost unless authorities take the time to screen debris for small pieces of human bone and teeth.

Throughout each phase of a case, the evidence must be documented and noted in the so-called "chain of evidence" or "chain of custody". Although every forensic case is unique or different many have the same processing requirements.

Case study: Vital signs of life missed

A 911 call reported a request to check on the well-being of two residents of a modest neighborhood. An elderly woman and her son "Buddy" had not been seen for a week. The officer first on the scene reported that no one answered his knock on the front door and requested backup before forcing an entry. The shift supervisor arrived and both officers entered through an open back door. The house seemed quiet as a tomb. A room-by-room search commenced and signs of prolonged neglect immediately caught their senses. Smelly trash and debris were piled to the ceilings leaving only small paths through the home. Their interest focused on one bedroom where the bed appeared occupied. An elderly woman lay under the bedcovers, which was neatly tucked up to her chin. They determined she was non-responsive and immediately called the paramedics who arrived from a nearby firehouse and reported her dead. Their search commenced once more for "Buddy." He was found shrunken into a mummified state. These officers realized the cause of death for the decedents could be murder or suicide and called the detective bureau to assign a homicide team. The homicide team showed up and confirmed the presence of two dead bodies. The coroner's investigator came to the house and a conference commenced on the front porch as the entire scene again was closed pending arrival of the evidence team from the crime lab. Noticing some movement inside the home, the seven law enforcement members looked through the doorway and some one pointed to a figure inside and said, "Who is that?".

The final incident report described the second call to the fire station to have the paramedics return and transport the now ambulatory elderly woman to the hospital. She was a victim of Alzheimer's disease and apparently had been unable to report her alcoholic son's demise when it had occurred months before.

Time must be given to note and properly record the scene's items and the relative positioning. Certainly objects within a room containing a dead person need special consideration both photographically and regarding what is done at and to the scene. Notes and sketches are mandatory to reconstruct what the investigators did during their activities to reconstruct what was done during a crime.

DETAILED SEARCH OF THE SCENE

Described below are the general steps a scene search should involve. Statements regarding general concepts and actual protocols are included. The details of specific types of dental evidence will then be listed.

First on the scene

1. Mitigation of life threatening situations and victim assistance. The preservation of life and property are foremost.
2. Suspect search and apprehension.
3. Determine possible witnesses to the event and document their independent statements.
4. Protection of the crime scene. The determination of its size should be a generous estimation. It can always be made smaller as time goes on. Physical barriers, signs and personnel at the perimeters should be utilized. The intent is to preserve all possible physical evidence within the perimeter. Keep from using *any* objects or devices at the scene. Remember that much evidence is very fragile and can be obliterated by contact with unaware personnel.

5. Do *not* bring any foodstuffs or biological material onto the scene.
6. Report to the supervisor regarding where the first responders entered the scene and what they do in various locations before handing over the scene to technical staff.
7. Take notes while at the scene and later include them in a detailed written report.

Second responders

Begin to form theories about the events that occurred at the scene. Interview the first responders. Walk through the scene with a mind-set that separates the normal circumstances of the scene with what may be abnormal or directly related to the crime itself. Normal details of the scene would include unmoved furniture, the position of personal items and the other myriad details of the scene type (inside residence or outdoors, etc.). Points of entry and exit should be established or possibilities noted. The presence of unusual odors, visible markings on objects or surfaces should be documented as possible targets for later collection. Use a mental checklist that keeps the big picture of:

- Who?
- What?
- Where?
- When?
- Why?
- How?

Support and forensic staff

Larger jurisdictions will have sworn and technical personnel who are assigned specific duties such as mapping, still photography, video photography, evidence marking and collection, biological evidence presumptive testing and collection. Smaller agencies may only have one or two support personnel for all these roles. Regardless of the total number of staff all parties should know what the others are doing and processing.

These individuals take the stage when all the preliminary processing and documentation has been finished. The puzzle regarding the totality of the crime scene should have a few of its pieces in place. The remaining pieces will substantially be obtained from the physical evidence.

THE COLLECTION STAGE

The amounts of physical evidence that can be obtained from, for example, a single-family residence can be staggering. A current case of note is the Laci Petersen case in Modesto, California. The police had access to her house for weeks based on a valid search warrant and removed hundreds of objects and evidence bags and containers from the property. In response to this task, a job description should be established for an evidence officer. This person will know *exactly* what goes out of the scene. Nothing should be missed.

Equipment for collection*

* Note: All items or objects must be separately collected and packaged.

1. Containers for evidence fall into four categories:
   - Paper and cardboard containers of various sizes for objects.
   - Blood and body fluid pipettes accompanied by plastic and glass containers or covered test tubes for storage.
   - Paper envelopes.
   - Tupperware containers of small to medium size.
2. Tools to remove trace DNA evidence
   - Sterile cotton swabs and sealable containers.
3. Adhesives
   - Hair spray or spray adhesives to stabilize burned tooth fragments before collection.
4. Labels
   - Labels, location markers and sealing tape – all containers must be sealed completely and labeled at the time of collection.
5. Airtight containers
   - For materials and liquids that evaporate.

Teeth and tooth fragments

The theory surrounding all the methods of scene searching is the timely, comprehensive and non-destructive acquisition of all available evidence. Dental evidence found at assault scenes are actually objects that should be considered for trace evidence. Tooth fragments or entire teeth that are broken off in fist-fights or by blunt force instruments (hammers, clubs, baseball bats, etc.) may challenge even an observant collector. Bits and pieces of teeth at an exterior scene resemble chips of quartzite and pale granite (Figure 2.13). These small items can be propelled during an assault and end up 20 feet or more away from the event, actually hiding under taller objects and furniture.

Once an item of dental value is identified the normal process should be to document, photograph and collect. Preserving hard material such as teeth (enamel and dentin) can catch an investigator by surprise when the material has been burned or nearly incinerated. These remains are extremely fragile and subject to crushing. Preservation via spraying the burned or nearly incinerated teeth with hair lacquer or poster adhesive adds some strength. Nevertheless, careful handling must be maintained.

Foodstuffs

Food is the most commonly missed item that may show evidence of partial chewing. This activity leaves cuts and serrations in the food that can have reasonable expectations of later use for bite mark comparisons. What is mandatory for the investigator is to remember that chewing also leaves trace amounts of saliva on the object. This saliva will not last, as foods have enzymes that denature (break into little pieces) the DNA strands present in epithelial cells combined in the saliva. Care must be used in protecting the foodstuff and immediate transportation to the DNA or serology laboratory.

- Rule #1: Never put food in a freezer.
- Rule #2: Never put food in a wet, warm or hot area.
- Rule #3: Use a labeled paper bag to transport. Do not use plastic bags.

Photography should be done first at the recovery location. Later, the laboratory (not crime scene) common technique is to remove possible saliva from these materials by swabbing them with moistened (distilled water or saline solution) cotton applicators (see Chapters 3 and 4). Once the biologist has obtained the swabs, photography must be performed again. Each photo must have a scale present to allow reproduction of the image to a life-size representation of the evidence.

Regardless of the outcome of the DNA profiling, the bitten object still has potential identification value. It is interesting that in both cases, DNA from saliva and bitten objects, there must be reference samples (saliva and teeth impressions) of suspects or people potentially involved in the case. If a positive connection is made with a person or persons, what is left is an explanation about how and when the objects came to be present. Neither method of identification lends itself to determining a time frame regarding time since occurrence.

Dental evidence collection at a coroners/medical examiner facility

The collection of dental evidence at a morgue or Coroner facility is under the jurisdiction of the medical examiner. It is common for coroner personnel to collect fingerprints, photographs, perform trace evidence collection and do sexual assault evidence collection. The dental evidence available at autopsy is under the control of the coroner or medical examiner and therefore, procedures are determined by those agencies. In general, the dental evidence collected is in response to questions asked by law enforcement such as, "Who is this person?" or "Is this a bite mark?" and "Who did it?". Bite mark protocols are described in Chapter 3.

Dental evidence and hospital/healthcare facilities

The officer who responds to a hospital to interview an assault victim should realize the possibility of dental evidence. Hospital personnel should be interviewed regarding skin injuries or hand injuries on the victim. Biting of a victim by an attacker can leave valuable evidence. The unconscious victim can not communicate the presence of injuries. The responding officer must discuss the case with attending medical staff. The protocol for a bite mark examination is described in Chapter 3.

ANTEMORTEM DENTAL PROFILING

In an unidentified deceased body case, the medical examiner or coroner should consult the forensic odontologist. Antemortem dental records hopefully will be obtained upon consultation with the family or friends of the deceased if there is a lead on the individual's possible identity. This will become the *antemortem dental profile*. Dental offices rarely have reservations about releasing original records, but state statutory power or a properly executed warrant will eliminate any reluctance on the part of the dentist (Figure 2.14).

POSTMORTEM DENTAL PROFILING

The dental autopsy of a deceased person begins with a complete dental examination. The physical features observed should be thoroughly documented on an examination chart that is kept in the autopsy report. Photographs and dental radiographs should be taken. The radiographs should be taken at angles and positions that mimic a traditional dental office exam. Large flat-plate X-rays of an intact skull may also be taken but these are not a substitute for dental film X-rays. This insures the latter comparison process (if it occurs) will have similar views of teeth and surroundings jaw structures (Figure 2.15).

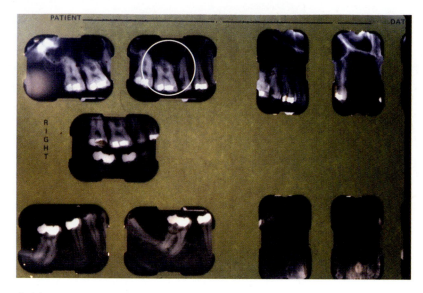

Figure 2.14

Investigators arriving at a dentist's office with a warrant or subpoena to seize dental records must know that it is dental radiographs, as shown here, which contain the most information useful for human dental identification. Written records are helpful but not usually conclusive evidence. The area within the white circle is seen in Figure 2.13. This was used to compare to the available postmortem human dental remains recovered from a highway accident. These individual X-rays are small and can be easily lost from the surrounding cardboard frame. The patient's name and the date when the X-rays were taken should be labeled and placed somewhere on the frame.

Figure 2.15

Salvaged gold crowns and bridges obtained from patients receiving new dental treatment. It can be argued that each dental restoration in this collection has its own individual shape.

Dental features (Figures 2.16–2.23) that should be documented by the forensic odontologist include:

- Teeth present and missing.
- Dental restorations (type and material used) present in each tooth (Figure 2.16).

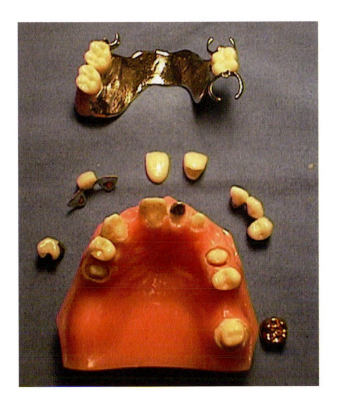

Figure 2.16
This array of dental work includes at top, a removable partial denture and below it, an assortment of bridgework and crowns.

- Fillings (size and position in tooth must be noted).
- Crowns (caps).
- Bridgework that replaces teeth.
- Removable artificial dentures (plates).
- Cosmetic coverings on front teeth (veneers).
- Root canal therapy (visible on X-rays).
- Root shapes and jaw bone anatomy.
- Tooth appearances that indicate habits (e.g. pipe smoking), bulimia or gastric regurgitation, injuries and postmortem changes.

COMPARISON OF THE DENTAL PROFILES

The comparison occurs after the odontologist completes the antemortem and postmortem dental profiles. The antemortem record of the known individual will be evaluated against the examination findings of the deceased subject. Any discrepancy that cannot be explained will make the comparison exclusionary and the comparison process goes no further. Some of these exclusionary discrepancies are:

1. The postmortem dental record shows a tooth present that was missing in the antemortem dental record.

Figure 2.17

The appearance of all the dental work in place on the demonstration model.

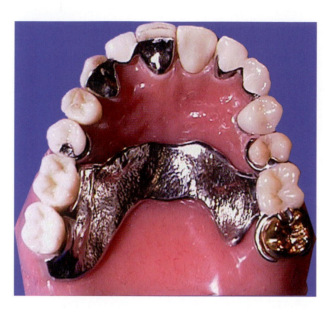

Figure 2.18

This is a porcelain fused to metal crown. It covers all of the surfaces of a tooth. The interior aspect is hollow and usually gold or chrome colored metal.

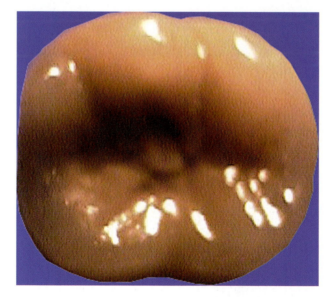

2. The postmortem dental record shows a tooth with no restoration (filling or crown) and the antemortem dental record shows a dental restoration.

3. The postmortem dental record shows a tooth with no root canal treatment and the antemortem dental record indicates the same tooth had a root canal performed.

4. The postmortem dental record shows a tooth with curved roots and the antemortem dental record does not support this feature.

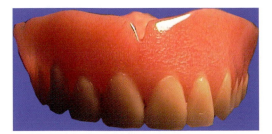

Figure 2.19

This is a full maxillary denture. The pink plastic mimics dental gum tissue. The teeth are made of either porcelain or tooth colored plastic.

Figure 2.20

The placement of tooth colored materials in teeth is quite popular in this age of cosmetic dentistry. This restoration is a porcelain inlay sitting in a plaster model. The inlay is ultimately cemented into a tooth. The appearance of this material both visually and on a dental X-ray will be much less obvious than a metal filling.

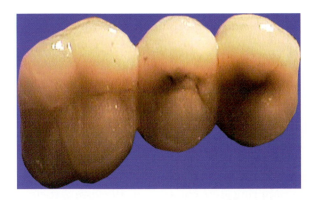

Figure 2.21

This is a three-tooth fixed bridge made from a porcelain (glass) exterior with internal metal framework. The glass will melt at temperatures above 1200°C.

Figure 2.22

This is a variation of a three-tooth fixed bridge. It is called a "Maryland bridge" and in this case is used to replace a single missing tooth. The "wings" of this bridge are cemented onto the back (lingual) surface of natural teeth.

Figure 2.23

This autopsy photograph shows the potential for tooth loss after death. Postmortem decomposition of the tissues around teeth will eventually allow the single-rooted teeth (front teeth and some premolars) to loosen. This makes teeth susceptible to being lost at the crime scene or during transport. It is very helpful to bag the head of the deceased, as well as use a total body bag in this case since the circumstances indicate the chance of tooth loss.

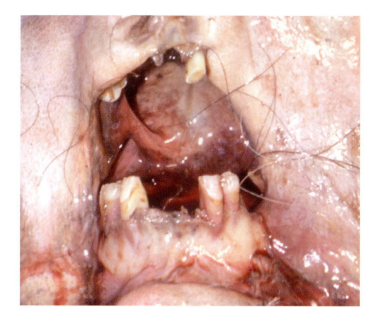

Commonly, when some time has passed between the last entry on the dental record and the date of the forensic examination, the possibility exists of additional treatment. For example, the last dental visit may have taken place four years earlier. The person may have changed dentists in the interim. Additional restorations, extractions or general observations will not be recorded in the available dental practice documents. An amalgam filling not present on the earlier record could have been placed subsequently. On the other hand, if a notation or a radiograph documents the presence of a filling and the clinical examination of the deceased shows that the tooth in question is in an untouched condition, the body does not match the name. Keep in mind that radiographs are much more reliable than written records, given the possibility of human error in charting notations. There is a tendency for some dentists only to record, in writing, areas requiring attention and not all existing (before starting treatment) conditions.

In some cases, there will be insufficient information in the antemortem records to make a clear comparison. Even with thorough and complete antemortem records, the possibility exists that there will not be enough individualizing information to allow a conclusive result. This is common in children and people without dental restorations. Perhaps the record narrative indicates that the patient only had their teeth cleaned and examined with no treatment necessary. In that case, the known and unknown dentition may be consistent with each other but the odontologist may not be able to make a positive identification. Again, the emphasis on the availability of radiographs is crucial (Figures 2.24–2.28).

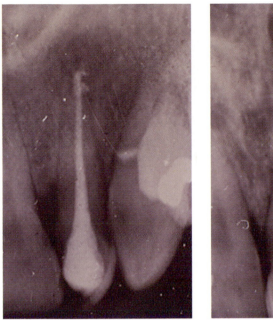
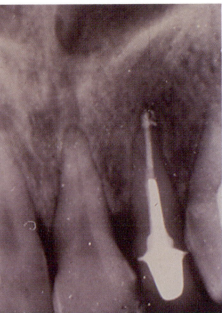

Figure 2.24

Two dental radiographs set side by side. The antemortem is on the left and postmortem on the right. The right radiograph shows that a crown and internal post was placed on the tooth sometime after the left radiograph was taken. The shapes of the root canal filling and other structures provide sufficient data for a positive dental identification to be made.

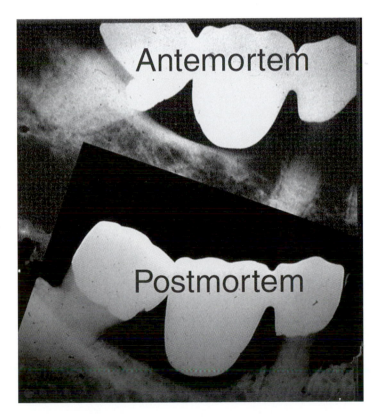

Figure 2.25

This is another example of a positive dental identification. The restoration is a three-unit (three-tooth) fixed bridge much like the example in Figure 2.22.

Figure 2.26

This is another example of a positive dental identification. The antemortem radiograph is on the left.

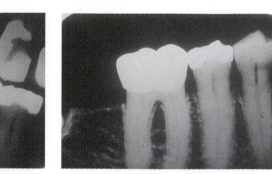

Figure 2.27

This positive identification has the metal filling from the left radiograph placed onto the right radiograph. The similarities of the two-dimensional curves of the compared fillings supported the final determination of identity. This case is described in detail in Chapter 7.

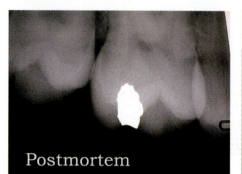
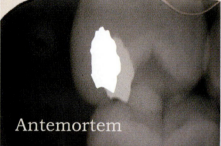

Postmortem   Antemortem

Figure 2.28

This is a digital comparison of an antemortem photograph and a lower postmortem photograph. The similarities between the two images supported a later determination of identity.

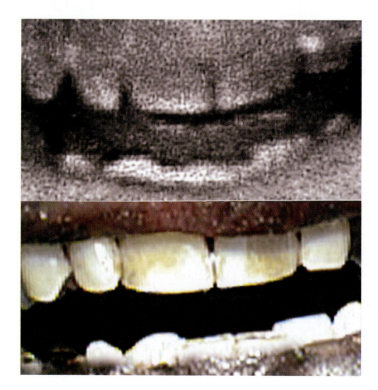

RECONSTRUCTION OF MUTILATED DENTAL REMAINS[2]

Postmortem tooth loss is common in cases where decomposition is advanced. Front teeth, having only one root, are more frequently lost than back teeth

[2] Law CA, Bowers CM. Radiographic reconstruction of root morphology in skeletonized remains: a case study. *J Forensic Sci* 1996; 41(3): 514–517. Reprint permission granted by ASTM, Inc.

Figure 2.29

This skull was recovered in a remote mountain area. It shows sun bleaching and weathering indicating environmental exposure for a number of years. The front of the upper jaw (white circle) shows unusual bone loss. The question of intentional mutilation was raised when other areas of the skull were examined.

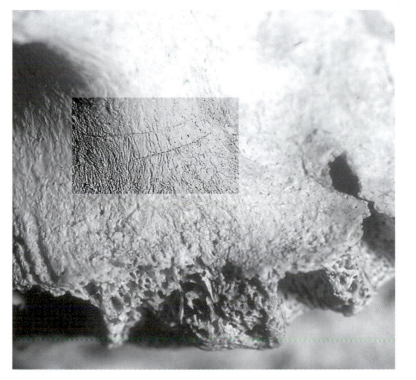

Figure 2.30

The digitally enhanced area within the box shows two parallel marks along the upper jaw.

Figure 2.31

View of the upper jaw (maxilla). The arrow points to a small remaining root tip. The degree of bone loss throughout this jaw is unusual. The holes in the jaw (sockets) are areas where teeth were present during life.

Figure 2.32

The sockets are filled with a material that shows white on radiographs. This material is a combination of a silicon dental impression and a barium chloride solution. It shows up white on X-rays.

(bicuspids and molars). Decomposition destroys the tissues and fibers that surround teeth and connect them to the jaw. Once tooth loss occurs, the jaw shows the residual empty socket. Intentional removal of teeth has been found in forensic casework. The only indication of this is telltale signs of tool marks in the remaining bone. The odontologist may attempt to reconstruct the root anatomy of the skull in order to develop possibilities of unusual root shape. These shapes might be apparent in archived dental records of missing person reports (Figures 2.29–2.33).

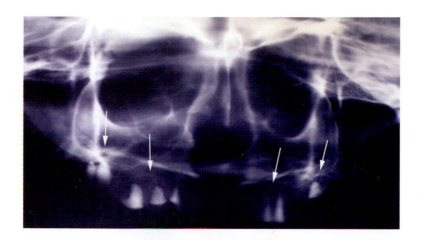

Figure 2.33

This skull radiograph (a dental panorex X-ray) reveals the shapes of the individual roots in the sockets remaining in the upper jaw (white arrows). This postmortem reconstruction can be compared with dental records from missing persons cases. The relative individualizing value of these roots, however, is low.

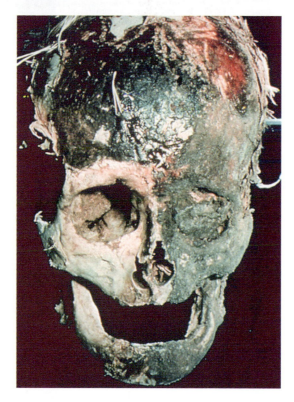

Figure 2.34

This mummified skull shows tooth loss that occurred long before death. The loss of teeth results in the jawbone becoming very thin and reduced in thickness.

POSTMORTEM EFFECTS ON DENTITION

Figures 2.34–2.43 show how dental information is still available from bodies that are decomposed, mummified and skeletonized. The dental work and bone structures can be damaged or fragmented but valuable information can be processed if the material is identified, properly documented and then collected.

Figure 2.35

An upper complete denture was recovered with a skull and placed onto the upper jaw to check for alignment and fit. Note that the jaw has no tissue remaining. This means the "fit" will be only approximate, as the dentures were constructed to fit a living person.

Figure 2.36

Complete dentures recovered with the skull in Figure 2.24 can be placed on each jaw to check for alignment and fit.

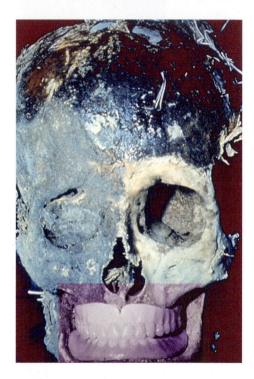

Figure 2.37

This set of complete dentures shows unusual wear on the front teeth. See Figure 2.38 for an explanation of the cause of this wear.

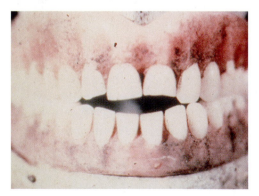

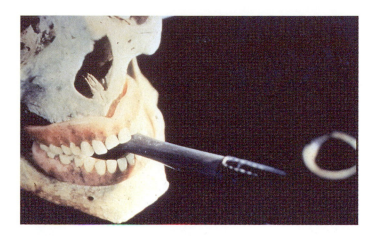

Figure 2.38
Constant pipe smoking can produce severe wear on both denture and natural teeth.

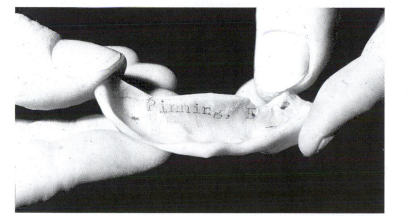

Figure 2.39
The inside of some dentures may contain the name of the owner. This extra procedure may be required by some States but not in others.

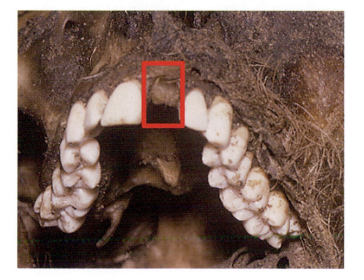

Figure 2.40
The red square surrounds a tooth socket that indicates postmortem loss.

Figure 2.41

These mummified skeletal remains shows extreme desiccation of the gingival tissues.

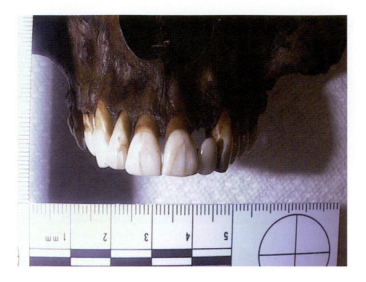

Figure 2.42

The white circles indicate stainless steel braces that were placed during life to treat a broken jaw.

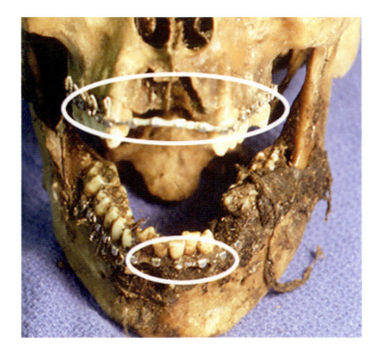

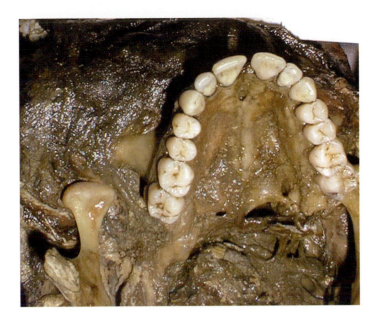

Figure 2.43
Decomposition processes
have no effect on hard
tooth structures.

CHAPTER 3

RECOGNITION, RECOVERY, AND ANALYSIS OF BITE MARK EVIDENCE

The material presented here is meant to provide the investigator with understanding of the appearance of bite marks, characteristics of bite marks, forensic terminology and the rationale of bite mark analysis as it exists in the 21st century. Contemporary bite mark analysis uses materials and techniques developed and familiar to the general dental practitioner but the determination of identities from bite marks is not the realm of the general dentist. Specialized expertise is necessary to understand both the strengths and limitations to bite mark analysis. These techniques have recently been aided by desktop digital imaging methods easily accessible to the forensic expert. Other adjunctive imaging techniques utilizing MRI, CAT scan or electron microscopy (SEM), will not be discussed herein due to rarely being available to odontologists.

Bite mark analysis is based on following two concepts or assumptions:

a. The dental characteristics of anterior teeth involved in biting are unique in all individuals and
b. This asserted uniqueness is transferred and recorded in the injury.

The current issue in bite mark analysis is, what, if anything, is "unique" regarding teeth. Not every person's teeth have been studied in order to support this contention of dental uniqueness. The notion, however, that a bite mark in skin "could have been made by a particular person (i.e. some one with teeth like the defendant)" is commonly stated by odontologists to law enforcement investigators, the forensic community and in court. Another confounding variable in studying bite skin injuries is that most show as only bruises and discolorations. These issues continue to challenge even the most experienced odontologists.

Bite mark analysis casework strives to connect a biter to the teeth pattern present on an object linked in some way to a crime or event. The general awareness of tooth-marks in skin and other objects is high due to popular print, film and television media. The general public and some law enforcement may

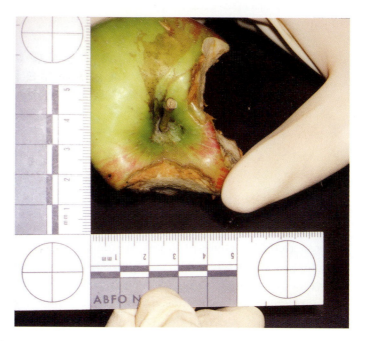

Figure 3.1

This bitten apple was considered valuable evidence and was recovered from a burglary scene. The two types of analyses possible on this apple are a) DNA swabbing for salivary DNA from the outer surface of the apple and b) the odontologist's study of the bitten edges of the apple's skin. The time since biting is difficult to determine but the brownish drying of the edges indicates a passage of time greater than a few hours. Drying of foodstuffs such as this apple also affects the shape of the bite marks. Because of this, impressions of the apple should be performed immediately after swabbing for DNA.

consider any "bite mark" case they develop to be a certainty in the quest to identify the biter. The ability of skin to register sufficient detail of a biter's teeth is highly variable. Bite mark casework indicates that many bite marks are not well-defined in detail and possess distortion due to the physical nature of skin itself. The current opinion of some senior odontologists is that bite marks can be useful in including or excluding possible suspects and the ability to identify only a single person as the biter is unlikely in skin injuries. Bite marks in other materials such as cheese, gum and more malleable substances possess more potential for identification. Figure 3.1 shows an item of food evidence obtained from a crime scene.

HISTORY OF BITE MARKS IN THE NEW WORLD

The first reported incident of bite mark identification in the New World occurred in 1692. The trial of Reverend George Burroughs in Salem, Massachusetts introduced testimony that a bite mark on one of the purported witches was left by Reverend Burroughs. Testimony of his biting was given by one of the women accused of witchcraft. He was convicted of witchcraft by the Court of Oyer and Terminer and hanged on August 19, 1692.

The 20th century judicial history shows Texas (Doyle vs. State) as the first appellate court to permit bite mark into court in 1954. The case involved a bite mark in cheese left at a burglary scene and a police technician, rather than a dentist, performed the analysis.

There are challenges in this area of forensic identification due to factors beyond the control of the medical examiner, forensic odontologist or police investigator. The first factor is skin being a poor surface to clearly capture the shapes of teeth making contact with it. The second factor is the common appearance and shape of human teeth. These topics are discussed further in this chapter.

SEQUENCE OF EVENTS IN A BITE MARK INVESTIGATION

The flow of a bite mark case involves the following steps:

1. Recognition.
2. Documentation.
3. Evidence collection and preservation (DNA and physical evidence).
4. Physical dental profiling of the questioned evidence (bite mark).
5. Physical dental profiling of the known evidence (suspect).
6. Physical comparison of (4) and (5) which produces either
   – a common link or
   – no link or
   – inability to determine because of poor quality of the evidence.
7. DNA profiling bite mark salivary swabbing evidence and suspect's DNA.
8. Communication of results to authorities and legal counsel.

RECOGNITION

RECOGNIZING A BITE MARK

The general opinion of most odontologists is that many bite marks associated with violent crime go unnoticed. This rationale stems from the broad range of reporting statistics from diverse areas of the U.S. It is apparent that forensically trained individuals in larger jurisdictions are more capable of discovering a bite mark wound or pattern than someone with little or no exposure to them. It is possible that larger communities have better trained public safety and health personnel. No formal demographics of "biting" activity between differing geographic areas are available but on a per capita basis larger metropolitan areas generate bite mark cases more than smaller population centers. The reason may be better training or at least a greater chance of recognition due to multi-agency

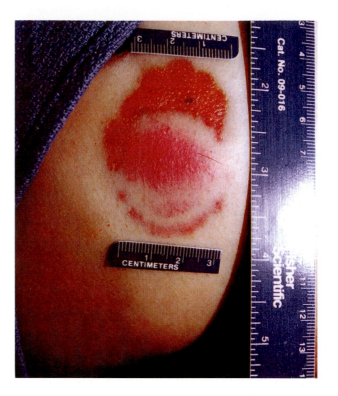

Figure 3.2

This image was taken at autopsy. The injury was located on the victim's back just above the shoulder blade. The placement of multiple 1-dimensional scales in the picture closely adjacent to the injury is important in order to properly re-size the injury to 1:1 (life size) for later comparison to a suspect's teeth. The picture shows the upper teeth marks on top of the image accompanied by considerable subcutaneous (under the skin) bleeding in the reddened area below the biting area. The upper teeth show as reddened outlines that give the appearance of a "scalloped edge" along the upper reddened border. The lower aspect of the bite mark (near the smaller ruler) show the classic "u" shaped curvature that a complete arrangement of six lower front teeth can produce. There is enough information in this bite mark to include a defendant as a "possible biter".

or emergency medical/hospital involvement. The responsibility of recognizing a possible bite mark usually falls on either law enforcement personnel or medical staff in hospitals or morgue facilities.

Recognition of a human bite mark is the first task. Figure 3.2 is a bite mark that shows obvious tooth characteristics.

The physical parameters of the injury can be measured. Figure 3.3 shows a close-up view of the lower teeth marks of Figure 3.2. The linear distances between teeth #22, 27 and #21, 22 can be compared to a suspect's dental features. Other regions within this injury can also be similarly measured, including angular features.

Hospital and law enforcement personnel may have a suspicion about an ovoid skin wound and call in the local dental expert for confirmation. Once it has been established that the injury is indeed a human bite mark, the expert will be

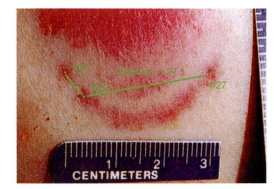

Figure 3.3

*Lower teeth were determined to be the cause of this bruising because the shallow "u" shaped curve
was narrower than the upper portion of the mark (Figure 3.2). The individual teeth that made this
lower mark appear to be similar in size that is a characteristic of lower front teeth. Teeth #22 and
#27 are cuspids and naturally have pointed tips when not heavily worn from use. The bruising
caused by these teeth can be more circular (i.e. round "dots") than the four lower front teeth, which
are more rectangular in shape.*

expected to document the injury. The final step is the comparison of the characteristics of the injury with those of the dentition of a suspected perpetrator.

The large majority of bite mark cases involve injuries to skin. Individuals having been bitten may be either alive or dead. In both instances, the evidence considered by bite mark analysis is subject to changes by the healing process and/or
decomposition. Training and personal knowledge of bite mark patterns in skin
and soft substances is necessary to achieve reliable surveillance of this type of evidence in everyday casework investigations. Investigators should be suspicious of
any marks or bruises which have characteristics resembling injuries by teeth.
The determination of an injury as being produced from human teeth requires
substantial information. Later confirmation that salivary DNA was also obtained
from the same site corroborates and sometimes eliminates opinions based on
incomplete patterns. Identification of a specific person is best done with both
physical and biological evidence derived from the same site (Figure 3.4).

PRELIMINARY BITE MARK EXAMINATION

The logic tree for the on-scene investigator or autopsy dental examiner involves
the following:

1. Is the pattern a bite mark?
2. Could human teeth be the cause of (1)?
3. Does the area allow swabbing for salivary DNA?
4. Do the teeth marks present in the evidence possess information sufficient to
   identify one person?

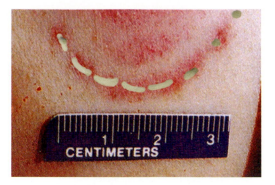

Figure 3.4

This is a superimposition of a defendant's lower teeth edges (the surfaces that would contact the skin) onto the injury. The correlation of the two is good, indicating that the suspect "could have made the bite mark". This opinion has to be tempered with the realization that the arrangement of these teeth is no means "unique". An alternative opinion that is more easily understood by juries is "the suspect cannot be excluded as a possible biter".

Figure 3.5

This injury was on the inside of a suspect's upper arm. The ambiguous arrangement of these bruises supports an opinion that they could have been made by any number of objects or means besides teeth. At trial, this case had experienced odontologists for the prosecution and defense who disagreed as to what and who had made these marks. Contrast the information available in this image with that of the previous bite mark case.

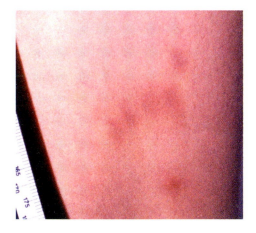

5. If (4) is "No": What features (if any) present in the bite mark are sufficient to eliminate specific people from the investigation?

   If (4) is "Yes": What is the probability of an unassociated person being "matched" with the bite mark evidence?

The importance of this investigative logic tree is to insure that any bite mark evidence be properly utilized. The scientific basis for bite mark identification does not give statistical probabilities. Rather, it uses personal opinions regarding the biter's identity. As such, bite mark analysis demands a conservative approach by the odontologist. Item #4 means that the "weight" or value of a bite mark must be considered in the light of the risk of possibly including an innocent (i.e. unassociated person) in a criminal investigation based on the odontologist's opinion.

The first determination of "Is it a bite mark?" is subjective, as casework indicates that many skin injuries from teeth are only partial "bites" without showing a complete complement of front teeth as seen in Figure 3.2. Figure 3.5 shows a skin injury that is not nearly as detailed as the bite mark in Figures 3.2–3.4.

This makes a layman's determination of a bite mark existing difficult. Even experienced odontologists disagree regarding this question. The idealized or "prototypical" bite mark shows the following characteristics:

> A circular or oval (doughnut) (ring-shaped) patterned injury consisting of two opposing (facing) symmetrical, U-shaped arches separated at their bases by open spaces. Following the periphery of the arches are a series of individual abrasions, contusions and/or lacerations reflecting the size, shape, arrangement and distribution of the class characteristics of the contacting surfaces of the human dentition.

This is a quote from the American Board of Forensic Odontology (ABFO) Bitemark Standards and Guidelines. Some of the ABFO's words regarding variations of the above description are in the next section.

VARIATIONS OF THE PROTOTYPICAL BITE MARK

According to the ABFO, variations of the prototypical (read: ideal) bite mark include additions, subtractions and distortions. Distortion of the skin indicates the dynamic nature of a situation where one person bites another. Biting force can be very powerful and the bitten skin surface may be twisted or on a location of the anatomy that is in a postural position that affects the impact of the teeth. The image of breast tissue in Figure 3.6 indicates how the anatomical location of a bite injury can produce a pattern that is a distorted replica of the teeth doing the biting.

There is movement of both persons during a physical assault with the victim's struggles being incited by the discomfort of the injury. Additions and subtractions means that in this dynamic situation certain teeth may not leave a mark or the same teeth may bite multiple times at or near the original bite site. Figure 3.7 is a model of a bite mark in cheese. The cut edges of the cheese are extremely clear. This is contrasted with the markings on the breast tissue of Figure 3.8.

The determination of why certain teeth don't mark in the injury is based on the opinion of the odontologist. The reasons for a "missing tooth" in an injury may be:

a. The biter does not possess that particular tooth or
b. The skin twisted in some way to avoid contact with the tooth.

Either determination is a subjective decision by the dentist, although it is possible to attempt to re-create (b) via test bites in materials (usually wax or silicone putty material) simulating human skin.

Figure 3.6

This image is of a homicide victim's right breast. The nature of breast tissue is readily apparent as the examiner's hand can move or change the shape of the small cuts seen underneath the areola.

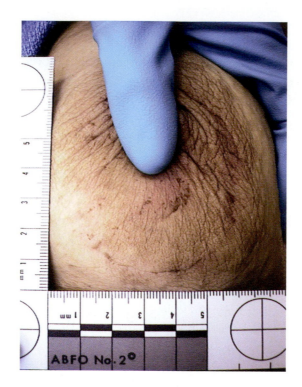

Figure 3.7

The outer edge of this model of bitten cheese shows the continuous outline of the upper four teeth (#7, 8, 9 and 10). Shrinkage from drying out (desiccation) is always an issue with bitten food. Preservation of the bite's details should include accurate impressions taken after swabbing for salivary DNA.

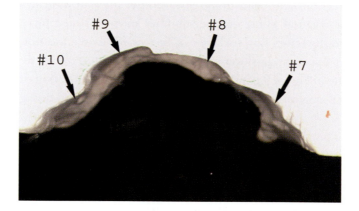

These different scenarios compound the task for the investigator because there are no dental minimums to determine a bite mark. Some dentist investigators have testified that two teeth have made dozens of injuries on the same person. This is an extreme and somewhat illogical opinion, since small abrasions can easily be made by many objects or may be an artifact of postmortem change and environmental insult (i.e. insects). What makes bite mark analysis a competent specialty is the investigator and odontologist accepting only reasonably high detail and undistorted injury patterns for a final analysis concerning a suspected biter.

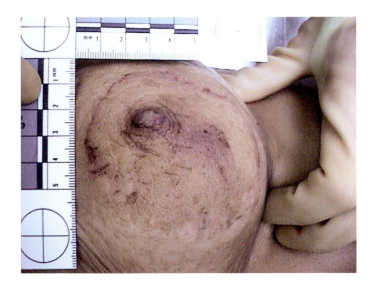

Figure 3.8

This overview image of shallow injuries on the breast shows how the skin surface may capture teeth marks as well as other scratches or small cuts.

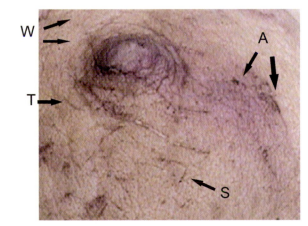

Figure 3.9

This close-up view of the nipple region of Figure 3.8 shows how normal skin textures lines (T), wrinkles (W), and scratches (S) and abrasions (A) all are present in the same image.

Additional features seen in skin injuries

- Central ecchymosis (central contusion) – this is seen in Figure 3.2 as the brilliantly reddened area in the middle of the upper teeth area.
- Linear abrasions, contusions or striations – these represent marks made by either slipping of teeth against skin or by imprinting of the lingual surfaces of teeth. The term *drag marks* is in common usage to describe the movement between the teeth and the skin while *lingual markings* is an appropriate term when the anatomy of the lingual surfaces are identified. Other acceptable descriptive terms include radial or sunburst pattern (Figures 3.8 and 3.9).
- Double bite – a "bite within a bite" occurring when skin slips after an initial contact of the teeth and then the teeth contact again a second time. Figure 3.10 shows a close-up of Figure 1.23 that shows this type of injury.

Figure 3.10
A "double bite" case.

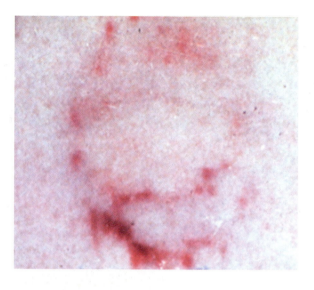

Figure 3.11

This is considered a "diffuse" bruising bite mark and is of little evidentiary value for biter identification. DNA swabbing of the injury, could direct suspicion on a particular person.

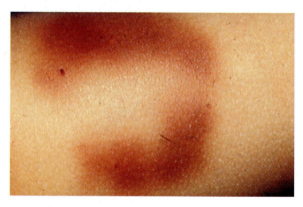

- Weave patterns of interposed clothing.
- Peripheral ecchymosis – due to excessive, confluent bruising (as seen in Figure 3.2).
- Partial bite marks
  - one-arched (half bites);
  - one or few teeth;
  - unilateral (one-sided) marks – due to incomplete dentition, uneven pressure or skewed bite.
- Indistinct/faded bite marks – healing in a live person will gradually affect the appearance of the injury (Figure 3.11).
- Fused arches – collective pressure of teeth leaves arched rings without showing individual tooth marks.
- Solid – ring pattern is not apparent because erythema or contusion fills the entire center leaving a filled, discolored, circular mark.

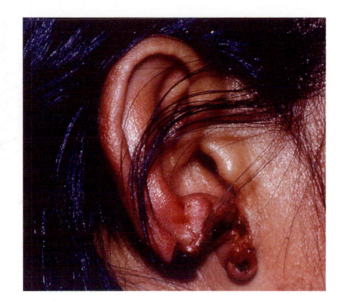

Figure 3.12
A living assault victim's avulsive bite mark injury.

- Closed arches – the maxillary and mandibular arch are not separate but joined at their edges.
- Latent – seen only with special imaging techniques.
- Superimposed or multiple bites – the Bundy case in Chapter 1 is an excellent example of this feature.
- Avulsive bites – this is when tissue or a significant body part (tongue, finger, etc.) is bitten off the victim. Figure 3.12 shows the damage of an ear being the target of a biter.

FEATURES INDICATIVE OF BITE MARKS IN SKIN

Human teeth are arranged in predictable patterns. There are dimensional variations in tooth size/shape/position between individuals that may be useful for forensic investigation if the bite mark itself is of sufficient detail. Teeth are used as a biological necessity in order for people to properly digest food. The use of teeth over the years produces changes based on personal activity, dental disease and dental treatment. All these factors arguably give each person a "dental profile" that can vary from commonplace to quite unusual.

Ovoid/elliptical patterns: A series of "C" (and facing each other) shaped abrasions or bruises that, taken as a whole, appears to the ovoid in its outline. This reflects the upper and lower front teeth in both adults and children. Some cases are seen with only a single "C" shaped mark (Figure 3.13). This indicates only one jaw making tooth marks (usually the lower jaw). This reduces the amount of information available to the investigator since a bite showing upper and lower

Figure 3.13
This "c" or "u" shaped injury only showed one dental arch (in this case the upper jaw). You could consider this bite mark to be similar to Figure 3.2 in detail. The area of excessive bruising (ecchymosis) is much more faint.

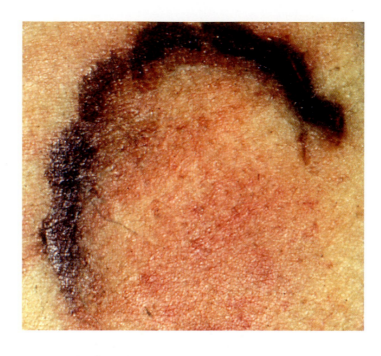

Figure 3.14

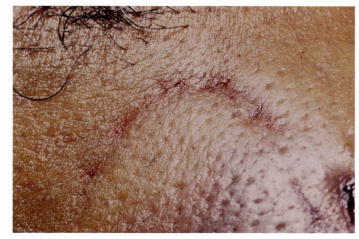

teeth contains twice as much detail. The absence of the other jaw marking during biting activity is explainable by a number of hypotheses such as saying, "Clothing can act as protection for skin during biting". The only way to prove this is to search the clothing (if available) for saliva and then, DNA. If DNA is present, the analysis of any bruising pattern may be moot.

Interrupted abrasions: This ovoid appearance can have individual tooth marks that indicate specific teeth. This is not, however, as common as generalized curved bruises which predominates most skin injuries. Figure 3.14 shows

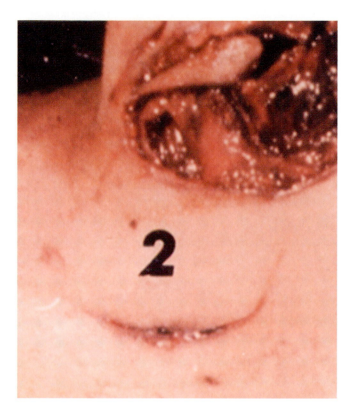

Figure 3.15
A forensic dentist considered the area below the number 2 to be a bite mark. The curvature is certainly a shallow "C" shape, but the width is much too large for human teeth. Careful analysis of the edges of the wound indicates sharp force injury as the mechanism of injury.

little in the way of individual tooth marks. The overall curvature of these lower teeth is quite apparent and could be used to include or exclude possible suspects in this homicide.

Continuous bruises: It should be known that curved bruising, approximately the shape of human jaws (actually, the front teeth), have been proven to originate from objects other than teeth (ECG pads, etc.). The diagnosis of a human bite mark, in this category of physical evidence, should be most conservative since bruising is seldom sufficiently detailed for human identification.

Misdiagnosis: In deceased individuals, skin decomposition and predator (insect) activity create injuries and produce skin patterns. The application of bite mark analysis on skin surface patterns in these cases is speculative unless there are clear and convincing markings in each pattern. What may seem as a "complex" biting patterns on the skin is actually postmortem and environmentally caused changes. Semi-elliptical injuries mimic the well-described "C" shaped patterns seen in an actual bite mark. Figure 3.15 shows the area labeled "2." A prosecution dentist considered this a bite mark but it is a knife wound.

LOCATIONS OF BITE MARKS ON HUMANS

The types of scenarios where bite marks occur can be categorized from the overall circumstances of the event. It should be noted that the bite marks themselves do not exhibit features indicating the specific intent of the biter.

- *Sexual assault:* Females exhibit bite marks on breasts, nipples, abdomen, thighs and pubis. Males receive bite marks on back, shoulders and penis.
- *Defense wounds:* Individuals being attacked can receive bite marks from their attacker on their forearms and hands.
- Animal bite marks.
- Initial animal attacks on humans focus on the legs and then advance to hands, arms, and the head and neck.

Cases likely to involve bite marks

Bite marks are generally associated with violent interactions such as sexual assault, child, elder abuse and homicide. Bitten foodstuffs left at a crime scene may be useful in determining the identity of a burglar, assault or homicide suspect. Criminals that occupy a crime scene for extended periods of time will use styrofoam cups, food and other utensils available to them.

Bite marks on victims of violence

Common locations where bite marks are found during postmortem examination are called *cluster bite mark sites*. On female victims, these sites include the breasts, thighs, abdomen, pubis and buttocks. The shoulders and backs of males are also cluster sites. Defensive wounds on hands and forearms of a victim should also be considered a possibility. It should be noted that bite marks could be made through clothing. Clothing should be considered a potential source of *both* physical bite mark impressions and biological evidence from transferred saliva. The biological value of the transferred saliva should not be underestimated as physical tooth markings on clothing or underlying skin are generally non-specific for an individual biter.

Victim bite marks on perpetrators

Circumstances during an assault may have the victim biting the attacker. This would be a self-defensive effort by the victim. Assuming a suspect in a homicide is detained for questioning and evidence sampling prior to a homicide victim's burial, the consideration can be made to take dental impressions of the deceased. This, however, is not a standard procedure in homicide examinations and generally is done only if the suspect shows possible bite marks noticed by law enforcement interviewers.

Homicides

The investigator should know when and where bite marks on skin occur during sexual assaults, child abuse and in the course of homicides. There is a "triad" of findings in certain types of homicides:

1. Strangulation and/or blunt force trauma.
2. Sexual assault.
3. Bite marks.

The initial investigator needs to raise the question: "Is the injury consistent with a human bite mark?". Early recognition by the investigator insures that the evidence will be properly collected during autopsy or during the victim interview. This question is necessary because, if the answer is positive, it initiates evidence collection and victim/witness/suspect interviews. The forensic dental expert will later look to the evidence for similarities/dissimilarities with any suspects. Regardless of the dentist's expertise, if the evidence is not collected or collected improperly, there will be no possibility of later answers to the first question.

Sexual activity involves biting activity in a noticeable number of cases. Child abuse (having either sexual or non-sexual contact) bite marks may be made by either adults or siblings or playmates. Sexual biting is seen between consenting or non-consenting adults. The ability to discern the difference between consensual and non-consensual biting activity is not well-defined in the literature. Certainly, biting that produces severe skin and tissue damage is beyond what a reasonable consenting adult would consider acceptable. In child cases, there is no capacity for the child to consent to any injurious activity.

MULTIPLE BITING INCIDENTS

Bruises of differing colors, with new abrasions (scrapes) adjacent to older scabbed injuries can indicate a series of separate biting events. This category of patterns is seen in ongoing cases of child abuse and elder abuse. In both cases, victims are unable to defend themselves and the perpetrator repeats the attacks over time. Faint skin injuries may be difficult to see without close examination under various types of light. Ultraviolet light creates an increase in reflectivity from subcutaneous tissue and is used in cases of faint injuries or injuries obscured by healing. Figure 3.16 shows a faint injury with a minimum of bite mark characteristics that was taken with UV photography and then digitally enhanced to increase its contrast and brightness.

TIME OF OCCURRENCE OF A BITE

Bruises in the skin of a live person change color as healing takes place. These color changes are different from person to person. Age estimation (aging) of the bite mark is neither a scientific nor accurate process. It is merely opinion.

ADULT VERSUS CHILD VERSUS TEEN AGE BITERS

Adult teeth are bigger and the adult jaw is wider (with exceptions) than that of a child. A young teenager, however, possesses some adult teeth and is developing towards an adult jaw size. When looking at bruising, the investigator must realize there are limitations in determining a cut-off between adult and teenager biters. An adolescent bite mark, if it is just bruising, can mimic an adult bite when the minor-aged biter is between the age of 12 and 17. In this age range, the baby teeth are lost and permanent teeth are erupting into place. This confusion can be caused by the vague appearance of many bruises. Bites in food, gum and other softer materials are easier to determine.

Figure 3.16

This injury may be useful only to either include or exclude possible biters.

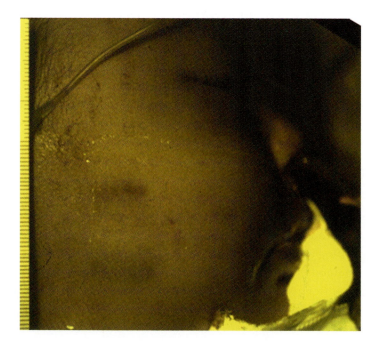

VARIABLE APPEARANCE OF BITE MARKS

The limiting factors in recognizing a pattern as originating from teeth are:

- the character of the material bitten,
- the power of the biting force.

Figure 3.17 shows the ability of a common styrofoam cup to retain teeth indentations.

The use of wax bites (e.g. wax exemplars) by dentists is very useful in reproducing a particular set of teeth edges. The models of a suspect are pressed into the wax when it is softened in warm warmer. Figure 3.18 shows the detail available from this type of material.

Skin does not consistently nor accurately reflect objects that contacts its surface. Bruising discoloration generally results from skin trauma and this both

Figure 3.17

A coffee cup collected from a crime scene could easily lead to the identification of a perpetrator. This image shows a bite mark of lower adult teeth revealed in styrofoam. The use of the ruler insures photographs can also be made that are 1 : 1 (life size). The front teeth (inside the colored box) show a misalignment that can be used to include a particular person as the biter. The investigator should also remember that DNA swabbing of this object would also be extremely useful in determining the biological profile of the biter.

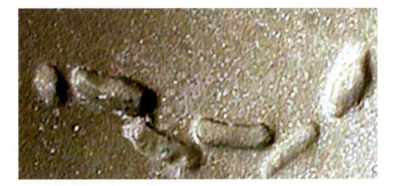

Figure 3.18

This wax impression can be used to capture just the biting edges of a suspect's teeth for later comparison with a bite mark.

changes and spreads over time. Foodstuffs commonly recognizable during a scene search also experience dehydration and shrinkage over time. Cheese is a very good substrate for teeth marks.

Bite marks may possess individual tooth marks that appear as a jagged or intricate pattern or show as an amorphous bruise with diffuse detail. Individual marks are considered markings produced by wear or accidental chipping of a tooth's edges. The term "uniqueness" is used in the dental literature regarding these features. This cannot be proven scientifically and should not be used. Bite marks of high evidentiary value should exhibit markings from a significant number of the six upper and/or six lower front teeth. Fewer than 12 teeth appearing in a bite mark diminishes the identification value of the evidence. Laceration or cutting of skin by human teeth is seldom seen. Animal bite marks, principally dogs and carnivorous wildlife, possess the dental characteristics necessary for deep gouges and lacerations. Figure 3.19 shows an arrangement of teeth that is not typical due to the chipping and breaking of a front tooth and the misalignment of the lower front teeth. The wax bite in Figure 3.18 was made from this person's dental models.

Forensic identification value of a injury pattern

A human bite mark may have a variety of characteristics and show considerable variation due to the following factors:

- Incomplete teeth marks without three-dimensional features.
- The surface bitten does not register physical indentations accurately (e.g. skin).

Upper and lower jaw teeth may or may be equally or unequally present. A "single jaw" mark suffers from a serious reduction of information and should be

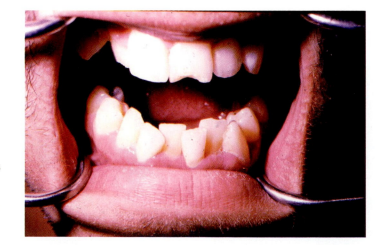

Figure 3.19

These lower teeth are obviously crooked. Also, their biting edges are not all at the same level. The broken upper front tooth (#9) has lost a large part of its chewing surface. Teeth with these features will leave marks in skin that show this difference in tooth height (i.e. length). The longer teeth and the corner edges of the chipped #9 produce more damage.

guardedly considered a bite mark. "Single tooth" marks are subject to considerable disagreement regarding the reliability of a positive link with a suspect or defendant. Physical features may be distorted due to victim movements and jaw movement of the assailant. Only one arch may be completely visible or only one side of both upper and lower arches. The anterior teeth are usually more likely to mark. Linear abrasions or stripe-like lines due to dragging can sometimes be seen.

Physical characteristics of a bite mark pattern

Definition of terms for the investigator:

- *Tooth width* is the longest distance along its biting surface (mesial to distal).
- *Tooth thickness* (lip to tongue; or labial to lingual) is the distance at right angles to the width.
- *Jaw width* is the distance, in the same jaw, from one side to the other. The cuspids (eyeteeth) are the usual landmarks for this measurement.

The fundamental step in bite mark analysis is the determination of which teeth made specific marks. This determination is based on the appearance of the features outlined below.

Tooth class characteristics:

A. Front teeth are seen as the primary biting teeth in bite marks. There are two incisor types: centrals, laterals and then the cuspids.
   - *Shape differences of the six upper front teeth.*   The two upper central incisors are wide and lateral incisors are narrower. The upper cuspids are cone shaped.
   - *Shape differences of the six lower front teeth.*   The two lower centrals and two laterals are uniform in width. The lower cuspids are cone shaped.
B. The upper jaw is wider than the lower jaw.
C. A bite mark showing the upper front teeth and the lower front teeth will show a total of up to 12 teeth marking in the skin.

The next step in bite mark analysis is the determination of which marks were made from upper teeth and from lower teeth. This is based on the following section.

Bite mark class characteristics:

A. The upper four front teeth make rectangular marks. The central being wider than the laterals.
B. The upper cuspids make round or ovoid marks.
C. The lower four front teeth make rectangular marks that are similar in width.
D. The lower cuspids make round or ovoid marks.

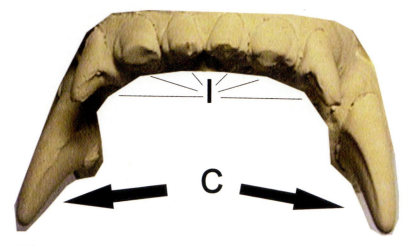

Figure 3.20

This is a plaster model of a dog's upper jaw. This shows the dagger-like canines (C) on either side of the six incisors (I). The dog was involved in an attack on an adult female who experienced severe lacerations from the long teeth seen in this picture. The obvious measurement to exclude a human as the biter is to measure the distance between the long upper canines. The typical distance, even in small dogs, is 50 mm or more. Human canines in the upper jaw are on average 40 mm apart in adults and teenagers.

    E. Gaps seen between marks clearly show four possibilities:
- The suspect has no tooth present.
- The tooth is shorter due to its normal shape or previous breakage.
- There was an object (i.e. clothing) that blocked the tooth (sometimes more than one tooth) from contacting the skin.
- Hypothetical scenarios that talk about tissue movement or biting mechanisms.

    F. Areas between known biting teeth that show significantly fainter bruising are attributed to teeth that did not impact the skin due to some feature present on the tooth. Difference in tissue contours might be another cause. This would be clearly seen in the bite mark photograph. The typical reason is the edge of the tooth is chipped or the tooth is shorter than the adjacent teeth.

DIFFERENCE BETWEEN HUMAN OR ANIMAL BITE MARKS

Large carnivore bite marks are seen in dog bite and mountain lion cases. The bite wounds produced can be remarkable in their depth and amount of damage to skin and underlying muscle. These animals have extremely long canines and a complement of six incisors plus the two canines for a total of eight. Figure 3.20 shows a plaster model of a dog's upper jaw. Figure 3.21 shows a California mountain lion jaw.

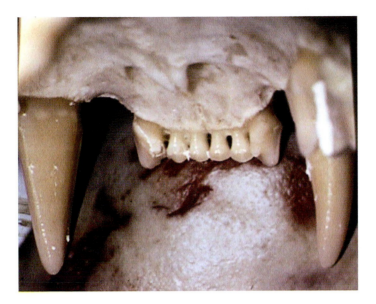

Figure 3.21
This jaw is from a mountain lion captured and euthansed after a fatal attack on a female jogger. This view is from the inside aspect of the jaw looking onto the skin of the victim. The canines develop the long slashing wounds as seen here. The smaller incisors (six as compared to a human's four) left smaller abrasions.

QUICK LIST OF EVIDENCE COLLECTION FOR BITE MARKS

Once recognized by an investigator, the opportunity to recover bite mark evidence and DNA evidence from saliva is time limited. The person who collects this evidence should have experience and have specialized training prior to doing actual casework. Casework indicates that in many situations this evidence will be recovered by non-dental personnel. This is *not* unusual as there are many jurisdictions without a staff forensic dentist. It is paramount that law enforcement or forensic staff properly prepare for these collection protocols and understand the principles behind these procedures.

RECOVERY OF SALIVARY DNA FROM BITTEN OBJECTS AND SKIN

The presence of a bite mark means that the mouth of the offender has made contact with an object. Such contact will almost certainly leave some trace of saliva. This can be an important source of DNA that can be used for identification purposes. Saliva contains skin cells from the lining of the oral cavity. These cells each contain a nucleus that possesses nuclear DNA. The concentration of these cells is quite high in human saliva and allows for recovery of potentially identifying information on who or what (animal) made the mark. The presence of a Y chromosome in the resulting profile indicates a male was the biter. The lack of a Y chromosome and presence of XX means a female was the biter.

The periphery and center of the bite mark is gently swabbed with sterile water and the cotton applicator tip preserved for later laboratory analysis. It is

Figure 3.22

The wet swab is placed gently against the skin and used to deposit the moisture evenly on the surface as a collection of small beads of water. Take care not to let the water run all over the arm as this may wash away valuable biological evidence.

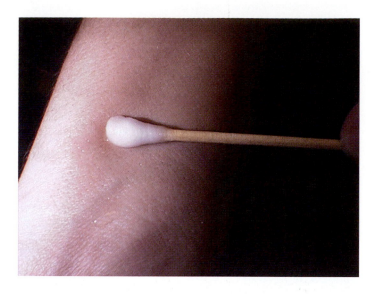

important to use sterile gloves throughout the following procedures. The specific steps are outlined in more detail in Chapter 4.

DNA COLLECTION FROM SKIN OR OBJECTS

Swab the area for DNA found in saliva deposited from biting, chewing or spitting.

Four swab technique

1. Wet the first swab with sterile water and swab the bitten area or piece of evidence (Figure 3.22).
2. Use a second dry swab and blot up sterile water from the first swab (Figure 3.23).
3. To obtain a control (background) sample, use a third and fourth swab to get a sample from another location on the object (e.g. styrofoam cup) or the victim (or biter).
4. Air-dry all swabs and place in labeled paper containers (Figure 3.24).
5. Store in a cold and dry environment before DNA processing.

PHOTOGRAPHY

A. Long-range view should be taken with case number visible in the frame. This is also called an *orientation photo*. The purpose is to reveal the general location of the bite mark on a body or the location of the object being investigated.
B. Close-up views with and without scale. Use the ABFO #2 scale if available (Lightning Powder Co., 1-800-852-0300). Make sure the scale is at the same level as the bite mark rather than above or below it.

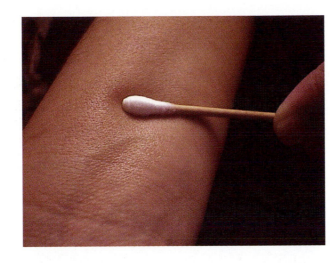

Figure 3.23

The second dry swab is applied to the skin in a circular pattern starting at the outer edge of the moisture and working with medium pressure towards the center.

Figure 3.24

This evidence-drying box protects the swabs from air borne contaminants. The swabs are placed upright in the plastic stand and then transferred into the drying box. (Photo courtesy of Lightning Powder, Jacksonville, FL, USA.)

IMPRESSIONS OF A BITE MARK

A. Use Dental Grade silicon impression material (polyvinylsiloxane).

B. Place a heavy backing (cotton or plaster) on A while it is setting. This insures no distortion of the impression on removal.

C. Take photographs of this process and make sure the impression is properly labeled and stored in a plastic container for processing by the odontologist.

WHAT THE DENTIST DOES NEXT

Once all the available bite mark evidence has be documented, collected and inventoried, the forensic dentist is asked to render an opinion. This opinion, initially may be just on the value of the bite mark evidence. Once a suspect or suspects are developed, then the dentist will initiate a "dental profiling" of these people regarding the biting characteristics of their teeth.

DEVELOPING THE SUSPECT'S DENTAL PROFILE

The arrangement of the front teeth of adult humans has features that may distinguish persons from one another. Suspects derived from ongoing case investigations may be examined and "dentally profiled" by the odontologist. This process involves the use of dental impression materials which are later used to produce life-size models of the person's teeth and jaws. The edges of these teeth are superimposed on photographs taken from objects captured from the crime scene or autopsy evidence. This effort is to establish the presence of significant similarities or discrepancies between these two evidence samples (suspect and bite mark).

OBJECTS BITTEN: HOW CERTAIN IS THE DENTIST ABOUT THE BITER?

Human bite marks sufficient to identify just one person are rare events. The odontologist has three levels of certainty or confidence that a particular person created a bite mark. The biter may be a "*possible biter*", "*probable biter*", or, "*with a high level of confidence*, is the biter". The opposite odontological opinion also exists, wherein the biter is "excluded" or eliminated from the investigation. Additionally, the evidence itself may be "inconclusive" as flawed or so fragmentary as to make it worthless for forensic physical comparison analysis. Do not forget, however, that once a bite mark is made, there is transfer of saliva onto the bitten surface, whatever that object may be. This makes the bite mark a dual source of evidence and subject of a physical analysis of the marks patterns and also the subject of biological analysis of the DNA contained in that saliva. Chapter 4 contains more information about DNA processing of biological evidence for DNA.

WHAT THE DENTIST LOOKS FOR IN THE SUSPECT'S MOUTH

Bite mark analysis uses features such as tooth size and shape, chips and fractures, jaw shape, tooth alignment, missing teeth and the lengths of the dentition to identify one person from another. The weight given to these features in establishing a "positive match" is the dentist's opinion. The equivalent features in tool mark analysis are called accidental characteristics. The dental equivalent means a change to a class characteristic (a tooth's general shape) due to events such as wear, accident or unusual dental restorations. The best opinion possible is when the dentist says, "Teeth like the suspect could have made the bite mark". The dentist then has to explain what is so special about these features seen in both the bite mark and a suspect biter.

AVOIDING BITE MARK MISDIAGNOSES

Occasionally ringworm, heel marks, defibrillator paddles, insect and animal bites have been mistaken for human bite marks on human skin. The experienced odontologist should recognize the difference and understand the fact that faint injuries on skin can be ambiguous if the patterns are incomplete or in the case of insects bites, unusually repetitive in appearance. It is essential that the dentist have a firm understanding of postmortem changes seen in dead bodies as well as skin pattern effects from animal and insect predation. Before or after death, insect bites will *not* exhibit underlying bruises in the subdermal layers. This is only observable through incisions made through the skin by the forensic pathologist.

WHAT MAKES A BITE MARK CAPABLE OF IDENTIFYING ONE PERSON?

The question of forensic value or "weight" of a bite mark is a personal decision of the odontologist. There are no defined statistics or guidelines that assure a bite mark is equally weighed by multiple odontologists. Expert narratives of dentists testifying that a "positive identification" has been made, talk about "distinctive, rare or unique" features in the bite mark that correlate to a particular suspect. It might be assumed that the mark itself, in these cases, shows a collection of single tooth marks. As the odontologist's attitude on what constitutes "uniqueness" is not derived from quantitative values or population data profiles, caution must be foremost in the investigator's mind on this subject. Calibration (consistency of results) of expert opinions on a particular bite mark is not always high. Adding to bite mark challenges are the layman (jury) and some judiciary having to listen to the words describing the odontologist's findings and then having to reach their own opinion on the question of identity. The range of identification value of skin injuries is very broad. The conservative approach for bite mark analysis considers the limitations to the techniques and the opinions presently available to the dentist.

Investigators should be aware that indistinct bite marks are the norm and it is very rare to see a skin pattern duplicating, in most details, the teeth of just one person. An example of an excellent bite mark case is described in Figure 3.25. This case shows how a person's crooked teeth can lead to an analysis that corroborates a victim's story of assault by an identified suspect.

The picture in Figure 3.25 is a good "orientation" image. It shows the general anatomical location of the injury. The shape of the injury would slightly change if the victim twisted or rotated her neck. Other areas of the body are even more susceptible to postural induced shape change. Biceps, legs, etc. should be

Figure 3.25

This bite mark victim rendered her attacker unconscious after a short struggle. The suspect was apprehended at the scene. The patterned injury on her neck is digitally enhanced for slightly better contrast.

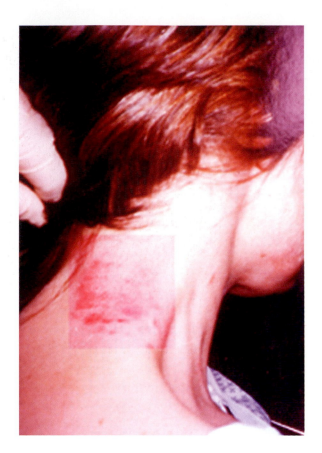

photographed in all possible natural postures. The neck picture below (Figure 3.26) shows how the investigator captured a close-up view of this neck abrasion and properly placed a scale. Also see Figure 3.27.

The forensic dentist can make a direct superimposition of the suspect's dental models onto the properly enlarged photograph of the bite injury. Figure 3.28 shows this procedure. This should not be the *only* method of comparison due to the plaster models blocking much of the image of the bite mark. The use of an exemplar of the suspect's teeth (i.e. an overlay) and the bite injury is seen in Figure 3.29.

EVIDENCE COLLECTION PROTOCOLS

The forensic dental community possesses a detailed protocol for bite mark evidence collection in the ABFO Bitemark Guidelines and Standards (http://forensic.to/webhome/bitemarks). Anyone tasked with casework

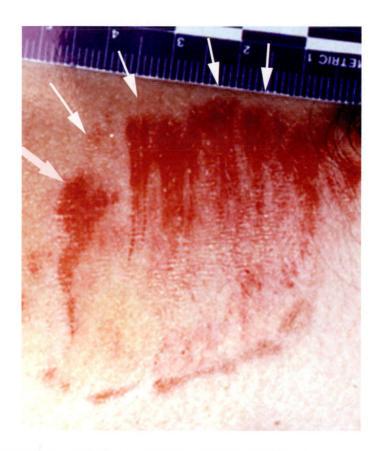

Figure 3.26

The white arrows point to the edges of the abrasion that reflect the arrangement of the biter's upper front teeth. The left two arrows indicate a "gap" or "non marking tooth".

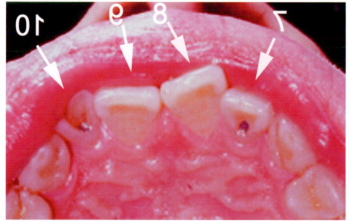

Figure 3.27

This is a picture of the suspect's (later, defendant) upper front teeth. The picture has been intentionally reversed to correspond to the orientation of Figure 3.26. The color is enhanced slightly for better contrast. The attackers' upper four front teeth (labeled #7, 8, 9, 10) show irregular alignment. Tooth #10 is pushed out towards the lip and is shorter than the other three teeth. This feature, where #10 could not make as much damage as #9 or #11, is reflected in Figure 3.26 along the left arrows.

Figure 3.28

This comparison with the dental stone models and the injury has the teeth edges placed slightly below the margin (edge) of the injury. Tooth #10 is indicated by the left black arrow and clearly is above the level of adjacent teeth #9 and #10.

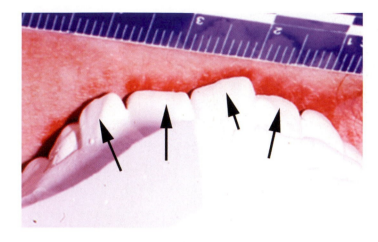

Figure 3.29

The edges of the suspect's teeth are placed onto the bite injury. This method can be done completely on a computer or may be done by hand drawing the teeth on a transparent sheet of acetate and then reversing it onto the bite mark image. In either method, attention to proper scaling and orientation is paramount.

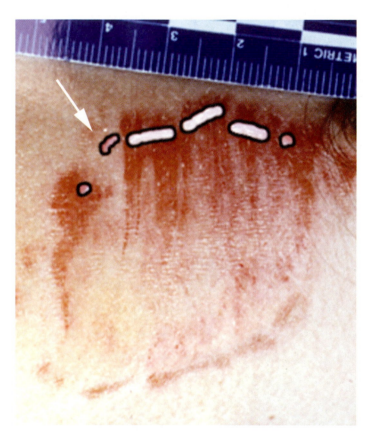

involving bite marks should be familiar with this information. This compilation of steps involving bite mark collection and preservation provides a meaningful and organized checklist for both evidence scene technicians and odontologists. A typical protocol stresses extensive photography with and

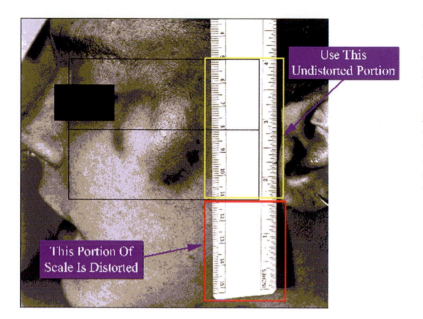

Use This Undistorted Portion

This Portion Of Scale Is Distorted

Figure 3.30
This investigator used a straight ruler to photograph the bite mark on the cheek of this victim. The red box surrounds the portion of the ruler that should not *be used to enlarge the image to life-size. The yellow box indicates the region of the ruler that is undistorted.*

without scales in view, taking impression of the bite mark site, swabbing the region and written documentation of the examination and procedures performed.

As skin is an elastic organ and changes with injury and healing, the methods of documentation and preservation of the bite mark pattern are of paramount importance. Materials and techniques must be of sufficiently high quality to minimize physical and photographic distortion. Given the curved nature of most areas of the body, camera angulation and lighting are particularly significant when photographing the injury. A scale must be included within the field of view to insure life-size accuracy when processing the photographs. Black, white and gray scales should be included to maintain color accuracy. Circular reference targets will reveal off-angle distortion in photographs that can later be corrected. The ABFO certified a standard right-angle scale that includes all these features. Lightning Powder Co. sells the ABFO No. 2 scale. Figure 3.30 shows what must be done in the situation when a scale is twisted or otherwise distorted during its use.

Initial film exposures of a bite mark should be long-range views without a ruler, in order to show direction, position and body part in perspective and in relation to victim and location (Figure 3.25). Subsequent exposures should all include the scale, be close to the injury and having the bitten object and scale parallel and on the same level. Care should be taken that photo flashes do not obscure the bite mark by "burning out" physical details.

RECOVERY OF BITE MARK EVIDENCE FROM THE VICTIM

The collection of bite mark evidence can occur at many stages in an investigation and may be done by a law enforcement technician, morgue technician, pathologist or dentist. Immediate recovery of this type of physical evidence is required due to potential degradation of the physical evidence over time. Live victims heal and dead victims are eventually buried or cremated. The evidence must be timely photographed, impressed (in cases that have actual indentations) and documented in terms of location and physical characteristics. Delayed evidence collection and analysis of a "newly discovered" bite mark limits the scope of data available to the examining dentist due to un-recovered information or biological evidence. The reduction in accuracy and reliability of any opinion results from early errors or omissions. DNA collection at the time of autopsy or examination is a vital part to the complete forensic analysis when potential bite mark evidence is of interest.

A living victim with a bite mark is a high priority given the changes that take place in skin as healing occurs. It is beneficial to take additional photographs on days after the incident so that changes can be documented and different details recorded.

PHOTOGRAPHS OF POTENTIAL BITE MARK EVIDENCE

Traditional forensic photography (color and B&W film) should be done before and after DNA collection. The purpose is to visually document the original condition of the evidence and its appearance after the DNA protocol and surface cleansing (removing blood stains) have been accomplished.

Interval photography sessions (1, 2, 3 days etc.) may be indicated on skin injuries that are both on live and dead individuals. Changes in skin color (from bruising) might improve in detail over time.

Scaled and non-scaled photographs

Long range and close-up pictures must be obtained of potential bite marks. These pictures should contain a reproducible scale. The importance of proper evidence and scale positioning will be described below.

Artificial lighting

Areas in a skin injury may have depth (three-dimensional features). The use of side lighting increases the ability to record these indentations via the use of low level (rather than directly above) positioning of the flash or other light source.

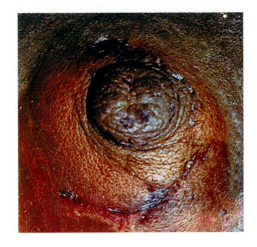

Figure 3.31
The curvature of this small breast is not reproducible in a photograph. This is why impressions of the region as well as multiple pictures with a properly positioned scale are taken.

Photographing curved surfaces

The human body has very few flat surfaces. Body positioning and muscle activity also varies the shapes of skin surfaces. The photographer must be aware that pictures of extremely curved surfaces create shapes that are distorted from real life. Incremental positioning of the camera above a curved surface (i.e. a breast) is the only way to control this type of inaccuracy. This is called "splitting the bite" where the camera is placed parallel to portions of the bite mark during multiple film exposures. A reliable measuring scale (L-shape or ruler) must be at the same level as the bite mark area of interest. Figure 3.31 is an example of a curved surface that will require multiple exposures to insure accurate reproduction of the bite mark.

This forensic subject demands rigorous adherence to evidence collection, forensic dental standards, procedures and a mature understanding of the strengths and weaknesses of the subject matter. It is recommended that inexperienced odontologists consult senior members of this discipline when embarking on actual casework. The documentation, collection and preservation of bite mark evidence contain pitfalls and traps that an uninitiated investigator may fall victim to. The use of an ABFO Board Certified Diplomate or an international equivalent should be considered for the final analysis of the dental evidence regardless of who originally captured all of the forensic material.

The primary source of bite mark evidence involves the originating photography of the teeth pattern. This process requires the use of a stringent photographic technique. The basic rules will be discussed below. Problems with capturing the image of the bite mark results from flawed placement of the evidence, camera and linear scale. Conclusions based on improper photography will be subject to admissibility arguments and possible exclusion in court.

RECORDING THE TOPOGRAPHY OF A BITE MARK

Bite marks occasionally exhibit indentations that can be recorded and preserved via impression taking. This type of bite mark has considerably more information than the typical bite mark that only shows bruising. Special categories of indentation evidence are foodstuffs and inanimate objects (e.g. styrofoam cups) that have surface textures amenable to three-dimensional detail. Contemporary dental impression materials that are silicon-based are highly recommended for this purpose. They have excellent dimensional stability and retain their shape over time and use. These impressions are used to create dental stone (much stronger than plaster) models (exemplars) that are compared to suspects developed in the case. Figures 3.32–3.37 show the steps involved in impressing a bite mark injury.

Dimensional stability of the impression material

The impression material used in a bite mark case must be given a reinforced backing before it is removed from the object (skin or food). This is to prevent twisting or other inaccuracies from being introduced through physical distortion. Acceptable backing materials are varied (e.g. acrylic, dental stone, or silicone putty) and can be added during or after the original impression material application.

Figure 3.32

This bite mark contains three-dimensional features that should be preserved via impression taking with proper dental materials. The use of adhesive backed ruler indicates the curvature of this bitten cheek, but can be difficult to use for sizing the picture (refer back to Figure 3.30).

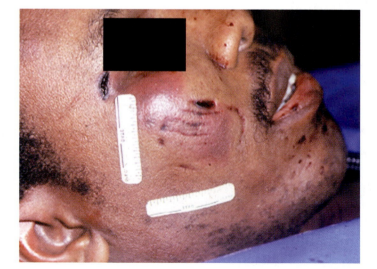

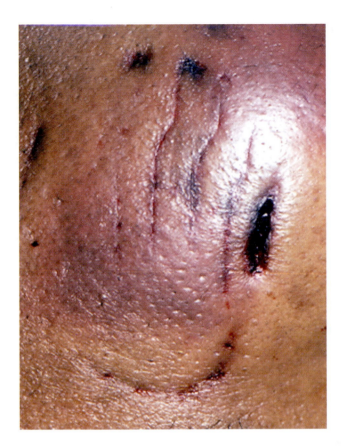

Figure 3.33

Close-up view of the bite mark. A canine (cuspid) tooth made the area of deepest skin penetration.

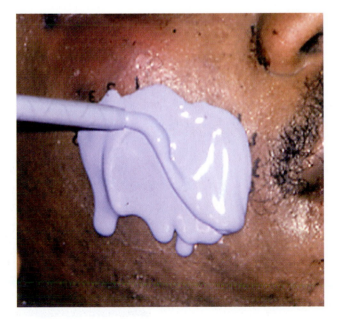

Figure 3.34

Silicone impression material is expressed onto the area of the bite mark using a dental syringe. The setting time of this material is variable based on the ambient temperature of the body.

Figure 3.35

Cotton backing is placed onto the impression material while it is still tacky. This will allow a plaster backing to be attached for structural stability of the impression material.

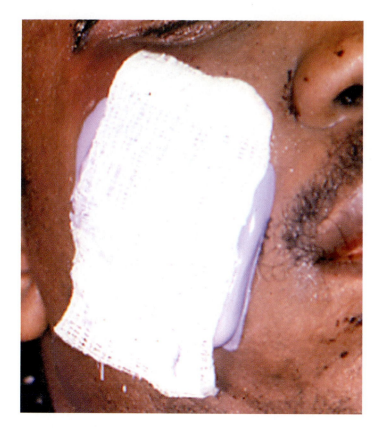

Figure 3.36

A dental plaster mix is placed onto the cotton backing. Once the setting is complete, arrows can be drawn on it to insure proper orientation.

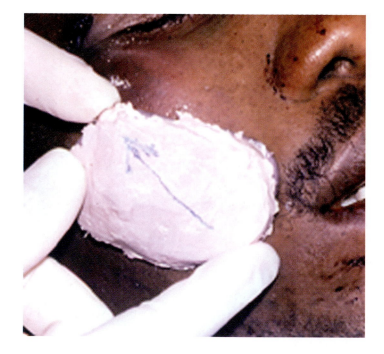

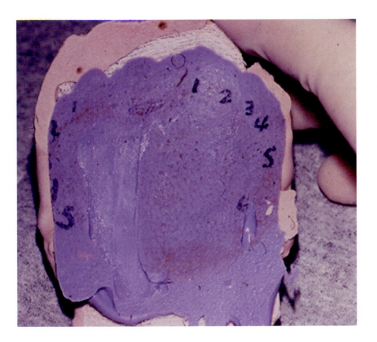

Figure 3.37
The interior surface of the bite mark impression after removal from the skin. Numbering is placed to insure proper orientation during later analysis. The final step is to pour a dental stone material onto this impression. This recreates actual surface of the bitten skin.

DOCUMENTATION OF BITE MARK EVIDENCE

PROPER RECORD KEEPING

Documentation of the location of the bite mark and the impression process includes:

- Photography of the bite site before and after taking impressions.
- Markings on the backing of the impression indicating.
- Notes.

Tissue removal and transillumination

The skin tissue and underlying fatty tissue may be recovered and preserved during a postmortem bite mark exam. This procedure requires the approval of the controlling coroner or medical examiner prior to initiation and should be performed after *all* other steps have been completed. The value of keeping the tissue is dependent on the dissection technique and proper stabilization of the tissue before removal. Tissue preservation in a 10% formalin solution is necessary immediately after tissue removal. The size and shape of the tissue, even with proper removal, quite often varies from either enlargement of the tissue or its shrinkage over prolonged storage in solution. Proponents of this method use the excised skin in a "transillumination" process wherein a bright light is placed behind it to better visualize bruising detail in the tissue underneath the skin surface.

LIVE VICTIM TESTIMONY

The recounting of a live victim with respect to the assault will be important in the analysis phase. The alleged offender may give a differing report regarding relative positions and actions. The injury pattern may show that only one of the scenarios is possible. Close attention should be paid to the position that the victim reports at the time of the assault. This is the position that the victim should assume when the photographs are taken since posture or body positional changes affect the shape of a bite mark. In a deceased bite mark victim, this type of information is obviously unattainable. Odontologists may attempt to reconstruct the position of the biter and victim via the orientation of a bite mark. In vague or diffuse injury patterns, this is of questionable accuracy and reliability.

RECOVERY OF BITE MARK EVIDENCE FROM A LIVE PERSON

Injuries can occur on people who do not die. The biter may be the assailant or the victim. The steps outlined above, with the exception of tissue removal, all apply to every bite mark case. A live subject, however, must consent to the examination in writing or be subject to a court order containing the specific steps to be performed.

LABORATORY ANALYSIS OF BITE MARK EVIDENCE

Serology or DNA laboratory work focuses on the swabbings taken from a possible bitten area. The best way to establish proper protocols is to contact the lab in your jurisdiction that will handle your casework. The best way to succeed is to plan ahead and establish collection and transport protocols that meet proper standards.

A forensic dentist should perform impressions, photographs and other documentation of bite mark evidence. The location is usually the morgue or Medical Examiner facility. Additional procedures may be performed with this evidence at the dentist's own laboratory. Transport protocols and chain of custody must be maintained throughout the process.

EVIDENCE COLLECTION FROM A SUSPECT

The collection of dental information and data from a suspect or possible suspect is extremely important. The following is an enlarged checklist that outlines the major knowledge items the investigator and the forensic dentist should know.

CONSENT OF THE SUBJECT

Once the injury to the victim has been documented it may be necessary to obtain dental impression from any potential or alleged perpetrator(s) or suspects. Either a signed informed consent document or a court order will be necessary in order for the evidence to be admissible later in court. Most jurisdictions require the form to contain specific information on what and how evidence is to be collected. Also, the odontologist should describe the procedures to the subject before performing them.

COLLECTION PROTOCOLS (DERIVED FROM THE ABFO BITE MARK STANDARDS AND GUIDELINES)

A. Dental Records

- Whenever possible, the dental records of the individual should be obtained. This will aid in establishing the suspect's dental profile and record of treatment. Sometimes a suspect will intentionally have front teeth altered or pulled after leaving a bite mark.

B. Photographic documentation of the dentition

- Photographs of the dentition should be taken by the forensic dentist or by a technician under the odontologist's direction.
- A scale such as the ABFO No. 2 scale should be utilized when using a scale in these photographs.
- Video or digital imaging can be used to document the dentition when utilized *in addition* to conventional photography.
- Tripods and/or focusing rails can be used at the discretion of the photographer.
- Extraoral photographs: a frontal full-face view and a view with the teeth in centric should be taken.
- Intraoral photographs: maxillary and mandibular occlusal views of the dentition should be taken whenever possible. Lateral views of the dentition may also be taken.

C. Clinical Examination

Extraoral considerations

- Maximum vertical opening and any deviations should be noted whenever possible. This measures how wide the person can open their mouth.

- Evidence of surgery, trauma and/or facial asymmetry should be noted.
- TMJ (jaw joint) function may be checked in addition to the previous observations.
- Muscle tone and balance may also be checked in addition to the previous observations.

Intraoral Considerations

- Missing and misaligned of teeth should be noted.
- Broken and restored teeth should be noted.
- The periodontal condition and tooth mobility should be noted whenever possible.
- Previous dental charts should be reviewed if available.
- Occlusal disharmonies should be noted whenever possible.
- The tongue size and function may be noted *in addition* to the previous observations.
- The bite classification may be noted *in addition* to the previous observations.

D. Dental impressions

- Dental impressions, following the ABFO Bite mark Analysis Guidelines, should be taken by the forensic dentist or by a technician under the odontologist's direction.
- Bite exemplars should be obtained in addition to the dental impressions.

E. Saliva Samples

- Saliva swabbings should be obtained if appropriate.

DENTAL AND DNA EVIDENCE COLLECTION FROM A SUSPECT

In order for models of the suspect's teeth to be created impressions are first taken. A stone mixture is poured into the impressions which hardens and duplicates the dentition in question. Photographs, written or audio taped notes and wax bite impressions will be necessary to complete the recording process. A DNA sample taken from inside the mouth (buccal swab) should also be considered as a means of collecting.

Special note is taken of unusual characteristics such as chipped or worn teeth, the presence of developmental mammelons (incisal edge with scalloped appearance) and spaces due to missing teeth, crowding and position in the jaws relative to cheek or tongue side. There may also be differences in the plane of occlusion from one tooth to another. Each of these factors will have a bearing on the injury pattern caused by the biter.

COMPARISON OF INJURY AND SUSPECT DENTAL EXEMPLARS

Once all the documentation requirements have been satisfied for both the bite mark and the dentition of the suspect, a comparison analysis is begun. Chapter 7 describes the entire process of comparison via digital imaging. The stone models of the suspect are compared to the photographs of the bite mark which have been enlarged to a 1:1 life-size ratio. The general arch size and shape is the first characteristic considered. If there is a discrepancy the suspect can be eliminated. The analysis continues in the absence of a discrepancy. Offenders may even try to alter their teeth by artificially causing wear or fractures in hope that they can eliminate themselves.

The models are oriented in the direction that corresponds to the position the offender was in at the time of the attack, as reported by the victim. Allowances are made for varying amounts of pressure being applied to the surface of the skin. Dominant features of the dentition are inspected first for concordance with the bite mark. Secondary features must be in accord or a reasonable explanation offered for discord. The wax bite impressions are used for comparison with the bite mark as well. Overlay transparencies can be computer generated from the models that accentuate the incisal edges and cusps of the teeth, facilitating the comparison process. Digital rectification of distorted bite marks' photographs is considered vital in order to control the physical variables seen in crime scene and autopsy pictures.

CONCLUSION

Bite mark analysis by dentists has 50 years of use in the U.S. courts. The best "match" possible between a suspect and a bitten object has been mentioned as "the biter has teeth like the suspect because …", wherein an explanation is also necessary regarding the relative weight or value of the connection between the evidence and a person. This chapter hopefully provides a person in law enforcement or other branches of investigation, the steps and rationale in the recognition, collection, and preservation of this type of physical forensic evidence.

CHAPTER 4

DNA AND FORENSIC ODONTOLOGY

BITE MARKS AND DNA – THE BLENDING OF MULTIPLE EXPERT OPINIONS

Law enforcement's role of being the first responder at a potential crime scene is a serious task. The later delegation of crime scene forensic analysis to scientific or forensic specialists does not eliminate the need for every member of a department to know the basics of DNA analysis. This chapter is written to tell the story about dental and salivary DNA. This material can be identified, recovered and preserved at the scene and submitted to a forensic laboratory for analysis. Officers should know what goes on in the "field" regarding DNA.

WHAT IS THE DNA PROFILING PROCESS?

Polymerase chain reaction (PCR) is the DNA evidence analysis technique utilized by most federal, state and local laboratories for DNA obtained from blood, hair follicles and body fluids. PCR is a sensitive, fast and reliable method of analysis. It requires very little biological material. Hence, the constant mention of swabbing as a potential way to obtain a sample of someone's DNA. In cases that have only hair shafts and dried bone, mitochondrial DNA (mtDNA) techniques allow a profiling of less discrimination (power) than PCR but one that clearly allows the investigator to associate one person to the original mtDNA. The DNA (both genomic and mitochondrial) differences between two people can be an extremely useful tool. A basic knowledge of evidence collection principles is necessary at the initial stage of collection and should be a regular topic for in-service training.

SCENE TYPES

Saliva is transferred through kissing, sucking, licking, eating, spitting and from sneezing. It is collectible from telephone receivers, cigarette butts, toothbrushes, bubble gum, used glassware, styrofoam cups, some types of lip-stick and foodstuffs.

Burglary scenes: The domestic burglary scene that has indications of extended stay by the perpetrators should create the question: "Where's the DNA?". Evidence of eating is indicated generally by food removal from refrigerators and opened containers. Coke and beer cans left opened and partially consumed should be photographed and collected for DNA and fingerprint review.

Homicide scenes: A prolonged visit to anyone's house increases the chance of DNA being left. A murder scene is no different. Saliva, blood and skin from nail scrapings are all possible evidences present at a crime scene.

Assault victims: Live victims must be interviewed and examined for the possibility of bite injuries or saliva left on clothing or skin.

DENTAL DNA COLLECTION METHODS

BITE MARKS

This information continues the discussion about DNA collection that is present in Chapter 3. It is meant to reinforce how important these steps are in any serious investigation.

Supplies:

1. Sterile cotton swabs containing,
2. Sterile distilled water or sterile normal saline.
3. Paper evidence envelopes or small cardboard evidence containers.
4. Sterile examination gloves.

Salivary DNA collection technique:

1. Take photographs of the injured or bitten object prior to performing any impressions of the evidence.
2. Use sterile gloves and take steps that prevent cross-contamination of the examiner's DNA (hair, saliva) onto the evidence site. *Do not* allow samples to cross-contaminate each other.
3. Four swab technique:*
   A. First swab – Moisten the tip of a cotton swab in distilled water or normal saline. Prevent over saturating the cotton tip.
   B. Starting from the center of the bitten area put the swab in contact with the surface using light pressure. Direct the cotton tip around the area and out to the edges. The purpose is to place liquid onto the surface that liberates the

* This is a technique described in: Sweet DJ, Lorente M, Lorente JA, Valenzuela A, Villanueva E. An improved method to recover saliva from human skin: the double swab technique. *J Forensic Sci* 1997; 42(2): 320–322.

        saliva containing skin cells of the biter. Be aware that blood in the area may be from either the victim or the biter. Avoid dragging blood from the periphery of the bite mark region onto the cotton tip.

    C. Second swab – Repeat the above step B without moistening the cotton tip. This step collects the liquid deposited by the first swab.

    D. Repeat steps A, B, in an area away from the site of bite mark interest on the human subject or object of evidence. This is called a "control swab".

4. Air-dry all swabs for 30 min. The drying should take place at normal room temperature and away from heat, sun light, and cross-contamination.

5. Label a paper envelope or cardboard container for each cotton swab. *Do not* place the control swab (step 3D) in common with the other swabs.

6. Keep these containers refrigerated (not frozen) until transport to a DNA laboratory is completed.

COLLECTION OF DNA FROM PERSONS

Cheek swabs can be collected from individuals and may, in fact, result in the discovery of some of the most highly concentrated DNA cells. A sterile cotton-tipped swab is scrubbed in the mouth on the inside of the cheek. No food or drink prior to 20 minutes of the collection.

Found objects

The following should be considered during the crime scene DNA evidence collection process.

- Saliva: cigarette butts, ski masks, envelopes, stamps, napkins.
- Perspiration from clothing and personal articles.
- Seminal fluid: oral, rectal, vaginal swabs, clothing.
- Blood (if the stain is visible, DNA results are likely).
- Hair.

Deceased unidentified individuals

Human tissue samples suitable for DNA analysis include bones (rib or long bones preferred), teeth, muscle tissue and associated property that may be found with the body (hairbrush, toothbrush, etc.). If no DNA is recovered from the nuclei of these tissues and hair follicles, then mtDNA may be profiled from the cell's area outside the nucleus. The power of mtDNA to identify a single person is statistically less certain than DNA from the nucleus (called genomic

Figure 4.1

Adult upper bicuspid tooth obtained from unidentified postmortem human remains. The DNA present in the dental pulp and root are recovered through specific laboratory procedures described in Figures 4.2 and 4.3.

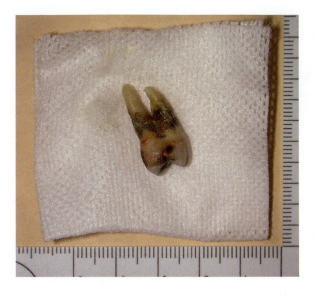

Figure 4.2

This machine is called a cryogenic grinder. The small cylinder receives the complete tooth that is flash frozen with liquid nitrogen. The cylinder also contains a heavy metal pellet that is used by the electromagnetic grinder to create a fine powder.

DNA), but it is commonly used by forensic biologists and is considered reliable by the courts.

WHAT THE LAB DOES

The process of obtaining DNA from a single tooth requires specific procedures that are described in Figures 4.1– 4.3. A tooth or tooth fragment needs to be pulverized before extraction of the DNA from other materials. Processing swabs of suspected saliva are placed in solution in order to wash the DNA containing cells away from the cotton tip. Once these steps are completed, the biologist then processes the extracted material through the PCR process.

Figure 4.3
The grinding produces a fine tooth powder that is then processed for PCR DNA profiling.

WHAT THE DENTIST DOES WITH DNA EVIDENCE

The odontologist faces a critical point when presented with a case that involves both the physical comparison of a questioned bite mark to a suspect's teeth and the potential of DNA results from related evidence. Nordby[1] has outlined the outside influences that affect expert testimony and noted pre-established "expectation-laden observations" as one such factor. Good scientific practice avoids bias and pre-judgment of data in clinical and lab experimentation by using single- or double-blind strategies that attempt to obtain pure data observations and control external influences.[2] The forensic dentist should be aware of these issues and perform the bite mark analysis without referring to or hopefully even without knowing any DNA results. Forensic casework is simply another form of experimentation, which requires independent analysis and independent interpretation by investigators. First, the odontologist performs the systematic physical comparison of the pattern injury or mark with dental stone models of known teeth. The DNA results are intentionally left unknown to the dentist. The important feature of this protocol is to keep the odontologist blind to the DNA results. This sequence of events assures the criminal justice system that the results are independent. If inter-examiner contamination occurs, the expert opinions will be linked, resulting in the DNA being independent and the dental assessment being tainted. The court use of expert testimony requires that participating scientists come to trial free of this flaw.

Police casework involving both forensic dentistry and molecular biology is increasingly commonplace as law enforcement protocols realize the power of

DNA profiling. Biological evidence from saliva, tooth fragments and tooth mark evidence, when recovered from the same crime scene, will result in parallel analyses that should be done by different examiners. In this scenario of multiple evidence analyses, the results of each should be done independently. These events create new issues regarding odontological testing protocols and examiner ethics. This chapter reviews three recently reported instances where both forensic dentistry and molecular biology became intertwined due to the nature of evidence found at crime scenes. This evidence may be derived from a common origin such as a bite mark on skin that is the site for trace amounts of saliva, blood or semen from a perpetrator. Possibly the evidence is tooth fragments recovered from a mass disaster. Similarly, an inanimate object connected to the scene might possess tooth marks and biological material that will be compared to physical and genetic data developed from a suspect.

VALIDITY OF DNA VERSUS BITE MARK OPINIONS

The forensic literature in the late 1990s contains compelling evidence of DNA analysis being used in conjunction with conventional bite mark and human identification casework.[3–7] DNA techniques are more tested than bite mark analysis[8] and have been adopted for paternity determination, biomedical research and serological comparison of known and unknown blood samples.[9] In light of the oft-quoted US Supreme Court's Daubert[10] decision, bite mark interpretation has been critically scrutinized by some forensic practitioners[11,12] and a few U.S. courts[13,14] but has escaped the obstacles applied to this decade's judicial review of DNA identification methods.[15] The odontologist, when asked to perform a physical comparison between questioned and unknown evidence in a case containing additional DNA testing, may end up supported, or possibly in conflict, with the biomolecular results. The various commercially available multi-probe PCR systems' greater power for discrimination and stringent validation process[16] may support or repudiate the odontologist's conventional physical comparison methods. A conflicting DNA result will, at the very least, reduce or exclude the weight given to the odontologist's results.

CASE HISTORIES

CASE 1[17]

A murder victim had been bound and gagged with commercially available duct tape. Marks of five upper teeth were clearly evident on the surface of the duct tape along with the impressions of the lower front teeth showing on the inner cardboard spool – apparently made by the assailant when he used his teeth to tear the tape. A forensic odontologist was retained by the prosecution to compare the pattern in the tape to a suspect's teeth. The suspect had two fractured upper front teeth, which compared favorably in size and position to the marks on the tape (Figure 4.4). Direct physical comparison and a video superimposition of the suspect's dental models were made with a duplicated model of the marks on the tape (Figure 4.5). The odontology report concluded, with a high degree of certainty, that the suspect's teeth made the indentations in the tape. Prior to the odontologist's analysis, the questioned tape had been swabbed and genomic DNA was obtained and profiled. A DNA report was submitted after the odontological result had been established. The DNA analysis confirmed the odontological findings by concluding the suspect's salivary DNA was on the duct tape. The suspect was tried and convicted of second-degree murder. The odontologist was not aware of the availability of DNA evidence until after the trial.

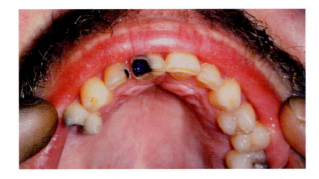

Figure 4.4

Defendant convicted in Case 1 on evidence from both salivary DNA and a bite mark in duct tape.

Figure 4.5

Tooth impressions in duct tape recovered from the homicide scene. Both DNA swabs and physical comparison of the tooth indentations identified the suspect.

Figure 4.6

This filter tip was recovered from the scene in Case 2 and contained enough DNA to eliminate a suspect in the case.

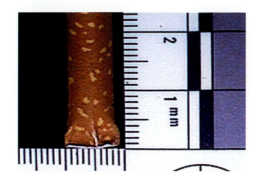

CASE 2[18]

A total of 22 cigarette butts were recovered from a crime scene as part of a homicide investigation. Small folds were noticed at the end of two filter tips that strongly suggested they were created by the edges of two teeth. The prosecution forensic odontologist opined that a certain suspect could have made the bite marks on the filters. The defense odontologist analyzed the same evidence and excluded the suspect. PCR analysis was then performed on saliva recovered from the filter material. The suspect was eliminated as the source of DNA on the filter tip (Figure 4.6).

REFERENCES

1. Nordby JJ. Can we believe what we see, if we see what we believe? – Expert disagreement. *J Forensic Sci* 1992; 37: 1115.

2. Burnette DM. *Critical Thinking, Understanding and Evaluating Dental Research.* IL: Quintessence Publishing Co., 1996; 143.

3. Bowers CM. Identification from bite marks: Scientific status. In: Faigman DL, Kaye D, Saks M and Sanders J (eds). *Modern Scientific Evidence: The Law and Science of Expert Testimony.* Minn: West Group, 1999, 2002, § 24-2.0; 26–27.

4. Lorente M, Andryala C, Lorente JA. Dandruff as a potential source of DNA in forensic casework. *J Forensic Sci* 1998; 43: 901–905.

5. Lord WD, Datsun JA. Isolation, amplification, and sequencing of human mitochondrial DNA obtained from human crab louse, *Phthirus pubis* (L), blood meals. *J Forensic Sci* 1998; 43: 1097–1000.

6. Sweet DJ, Hildebrand D. Saliva from cheese bite yields DNA profile of burglar: a case report. *Int J Legal Med* 1999; 112(3): 201–203.

7. Sweet DJ, Shutter GO. Analysis of salivary DNA evidence from a bite mark on a body submerged in water. *J Forensic Sci* 1999; 44(5): 1069–1072.

8. Whittaker DK. Some laboratory studies on the accuracy of bite mark comparison. *Int J For Dent* 1975; 25: 166.

9. Budowle B. The application of PCR to forensic science. In: Mullis KB et al (eds). *The Polymerase Chain Reaction* 1994, Birkhauser Verlag AG, Basel, Switzerland.

10. 509 U.S. 579, 113 S.C. 2786, 125 LED.2d 459 (1993). This United States Supreme Court decision affected the admissibility of scientific evidence. Prior to Daubert, the admission of expert opinion required only its adherence to a "general acceptance" approval from the relevant community of scientists. After Daubert, this one standard of judicial review was expanded to include the particular discipline's scientific data, testing of error rates, and the "falsifiability" of data.

11. Bowers CM. A statement why court opinions on bite mark analysis should be limited [comment]. *Newsl Am Board Forensic Odontol* 1996; 4: 5.

12. Rothwell B. Bite marks in forensic dentistry: a review of legal, scientific issues. *J Am Dent Assn* 1995; 124: 228.

13. State *v.* Hodgson, 512 N.W.2d 95 (Minn. 1994). The court didn't consider bite mark analysis a novel or emerging type of science and the Daubert standard did not apply in the lower state court.

14. Howard *v.* State, 701 So.2d 274, 288 (Miss. 1997). In part, the Mississippi Supreme Court stated "there is little consensus in the scientific community on the number of points which must match before any positive identification can be announced."

15. Thompson WC. Evaluating the admissibility of new genetic identification tests: lessons from the DNA war. *J Crim Law Criminol* 1993; 84(1): 22–104.

16. Fregeau C, Bowen KL, Fourney RM. Validation of highly polymorphic fluorescent multiplex short tandem repeat systems using two generations of DNA sequencers. *J Forensic Sci* 1999; 44: 133–163.

17. State *v.* Wesley White, Case no. 5941815-3, Contra Costa County, California, Superior Court (1998).

18. State *v.* Brenner, San Bernardino County Municipal Court, East Desert District Case no. FMB01563 (Jan. 1998), San Bernardino, California.

CHAPTER 5

PHYSICAL ABUSE AND FORENSIC DENTISTRY: THE DIAGNOSIS OF VIOLENCE

This chapter provides a general review of the physical characteristics of abuse and neglect with an emphasis on the dental aspects of investigation. Some recent statistics from US government reports of abuse are included but sociological aspects of these occurrences will not be discussed due to the number of references on these subject and the amount of depth required to adequately cover these topics. The glossary at the end of this chapter includes abuse terminology and definitions considered important for investigators.

WHAT IS ABUSE?

CHILD ABUSE

Recognizing child abuse and neglect

Child abuse is given general and broad descriptions. These include physical abuse, physical neglect, sexual abuse and emotional abuse of a child below 18 years of age by an adult. The perpetrator may be a parent, another family member, unrelated adult or caregiver. Abused or neglected children have their physical or psychological health or development harmed by the actions or omissions (failure to act) of another.

Actually, abuse has four categories. They may all exist in the same case or only individually.

The first is *physical abuse*:

- Is not considered an accident.
- The child may be withdrawn or overtly afraid of parent.
- Ranges from small bruises to cigarette burns, lacerations, ear pulling, torn lips and other injuries.
- See Figure 5.1 for an obvious example of child abuse.

Forensic Dental Evidence
ISBN: 0-1212-1042-1

Figure 5.1

This digital enhancement of a bite mark injury on an infant is a prime example of child abuse. The size of the teeth (adult versus child) of this mark would be critical in determining whether an adult or another child was the biter. DNA swabbing should be done immediately upon law enforcement's contact with the child. Please refer to the DNA collection protocols in Chapter 3 and 4.

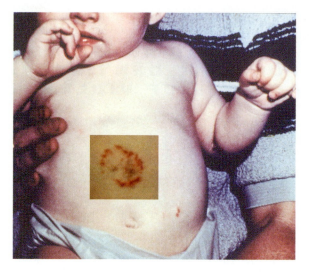

The second aspect is *physical neglect*:

- Depriving the child of clothing, hygiene, medical care and supervision.
- An example is a chronically unsupervised young child, or a child left to wander in public places. The investigator has to balance their decision on whether the parent knew or should have known the child was alone. Poor hygiene, poor nutrition or inadequate clothing for weather conditions may be basis to explore the parent's ability to adequately care for the child.

The third aspect is *sexual abuse*:

- Physical intercourse, fondling or exploiting a child for sexual purposes.
- The child may describe pain or discomfort in their genital or rectal area. This must be investigated by trained medical personnel to determine its cause.

The fourth aspect is *emotional abuse*:

- Constant, unrelenting criticism of the child.
- Parenting that is lacking in affection and care.

ELDER PHYSICAL ABUSE

The gamut of abuse extends to the aged as well and the above categories of abuse types still applies. Abuse is any physical pain or injury that is purposely inflicted upon an elder. The perpetrator must be mentally competent and generally is a caregiver or relative. This includes beatings, forceful contact (slapping or punching), sexual assault, unreasonable physical restraint and prolonged deprivation of health care, food or water.

Types and percentages of elder abuse in the US in 1996:

- Neglect: 50%.
- Sexual abuse: 0.3%.
- Emotional/mental abuse: 35.4%.
- Physical abuse: 25%.
- Financial exploitation: 30%.

SPOUSAL ABUSE

Different forms of spousal abuse

Abuse can be physical, psychological, sexual or financial. Once again, the abuse patterns exist just as in elder abuse. A person may experience more than one kind of abuse. Physical abuse can include hitting, punching, slapping, pushing, pinching, kicking, burning, shooting, stabbing or cutting. Physical abuse is legally known as assault. A person commits assault when they intentionally use force or try to use force against a person.

WHAT IS NOT CHILD, SPOUSAL OR ELDER ABUSE

- Injuries caused by altercations between children or adults who mutually agree to combat one another.
- Sexual contact between minors both of whom are under the age of 14 (most jurisdictions).

STATISTICAL SUMMARY

The numbers and frequencies of law enforcement cases involving these issues in the U.S. are large.[1]

Abuse and maltreatment cases of children:

- Year: 2001, Place: United States.
- Number of agency referrals for possible abuse: over 3 million.
- Percentage investigated: 2/3 (67%).
- Number of cases confirmed as abuse or neglect: almost 1 million.
- Percentage found to be maltreatment: 21%.
- Percentage determined to be groundless: 57%.
- Estimated 1,000–2,000 child abuse and neglect fatalities per year.

[1] Third National Incidence Study of Child Abuse and Neglect, 1996, US Health and Human Services Administration.

Approximately 903,000 children were victims of abuse and neglect during 2001. This national estimate is based on data from 51 states. In these states, 12.4 children for every 1,000 children in the population were victims of abuse or neglect. A child was counted each time he or she was found to be a victim of maltreatment. The victimization rate of 12.4 in 2001 is comparable to the rate of 12.2 in 2000 per 1,000 children in the population, especially given that the child population base numbers were estimated. Both the rate in 2000 and 2001 are lower than the rate in 1998. The rate in 1999 is considered unduly influenced by the census population estimates.

- Children who had been victimized prior to a first report in 2001 were more than twice as likely to experience recurrence compared to children without a prior history of victimization.

- In comparison to children who experienced physical abuse, children who were neglected were 44 percent more likely to experience recurrence. Children who experienced additional types of maltreatment were 17 percent more likely to experience recurrence and children who had experienced multiple forms of maltreatment were 14 percent more likely to experience recurrence than physically maltreated children were.

- Children who received post-investigation services were 50 percent more likely to be maltreated again; children placed in foster care were 23 percent more likely to experience abuse and neglect than children who were not placed.

- The youngest children (from birth through age 3) were most likely to experience a recurrence of maltreatment.

- Compared to White children, African-American children were 17 percent less likely to experience recurrence. Children of Hispanic ethnicity were 20 percent less likely and Asian Pacific Islanders were 27 percent less likely to experience recurrence than White children.

  - The estimated number of physically abused children rose from 311,500 to 614,100 (a 97% increase);

  - The estimated number of sexually abused children increased from an estimated 133,600 children to 300,200 (a 125% increase);

  - The more recent estimate of the number of emotionally abused children was 183 percent higher than the previous estimate (188,100 in 1986 versus 532,200 in 1993);

  - The estimated number of physically neglected children increased from 507,700 to 1,335,100 (a 163% increase); and

  - The estimated number of emotionally neglected children nearly tripled in the interval between the studies, rising from 203,000 in 1986 to 585,100 in 1993 (a 188% increase).[2]

[2] Report: Victims Child Maltreatment 2001, United States Health and Human Services Administration.

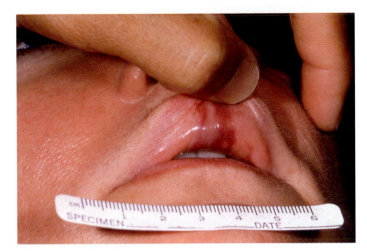

Figure 5.2
The inner lining of the upper and lower lip can show evidence of physical trauma that is invisible on the outer surface of the face. This injury occurred during a domestic assault by a spouse.

ABUSE CASES WITH POSSIBLE DENTAL EVIDENCE

The originating agency in a case of abuse assumes the responsibility of pursuing a fair analysis of the facts and findings from the circumstances of each case. This includes compiling a complete history of each case, documenting interviews and doing, in most cases, an initial physical assessment with the aid of health care experts. Investigators should keep in mind there are some injuries that are *not* specific signs of abuse and require a differential diagnosis that requires judgment and extensive experience to assess properly. Dentists can be brought into these cases to assess various types of injuries on either adults or children. Quite possibly, other health professionals (nurses and physicians) may reach independent opinions regarding physical injuries involving the head and facial areas as well as determining the presence of bite marks.

Child and elder abuse injuries can range from mild to extreme. Dental injuries by themselves are rarely fatal but they do form an aspect of the constellation of head, face and neck injuries that are indicative of physical injury at the hands of another human being.

The face, head and the mouth are sites of a large percentage (generally accepted to be over 50% of reported cases) of injuries in young children and adults subject to assaults. Multiple injuries, both externally and inside the child or adult's mouth, should be considered in any investigation. The victim's head and face appear to be a favorite target for physical assaults (Figure 5.2).

GENERAL DEFINITIONS OF ABUSE AND NEGLECT

The general terms describing abuse are strictly legal in form. Child abuse is considered but may not be limited to, an act or failure to act on the part of a custodial adult that results in death, serious physical or psychological harm, sexual abuse or exploitation. Types of abuse can include emotional injury, permitting a child to be in circumstances which are emotional or mentally harmful, lack of reasonable action to protect physical or emotional harm, sexual conduct harmful to the child physically or emotionally and acts which result in substantial harm to a child or a threat of substantial harm.

Neglect of a child includes leaving a child in a circumstance where the child is exposed to substantial risk of physical or emotional harm. Also included are, any failure to seek and obtain medical care for a child and the failure to provide food, clothing and shelter. Finally, the failure to remove a child from exposure to possible sexual or physical abuse is contained in the definition of neglect.

CULTURAL DEFINITIONS OF ABUSE

The standard of care for the determination of child, spousal or elder abuse relies heavily on common sense observations by the investigator and support from independent analysis by properly trained personnel. What is or is *not* abuse can develop into a battle of opinion based on assumptions that lack secondary corroboration when the physical signs are ambiguous.

TYPES OF MALTREATMENT

[3]Id

Figure 5.3

Victimization rates by maltreatment type, 1997–2001.

During 2001, 59.2 percent of victims suffered neglect (including medical neglect); 18.6 percent were physically abused; 9.6 percent were sexually abused and 6.8 percent were emotionally or psychologically maltreated. Figure 5.3[3] shows the distribution of child abuse type for a 4-year period. In addition, 19.5 percent of victims were associated with "Other" type of maltreatment, which was not coded

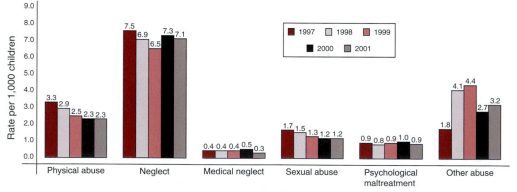

as one of the main types of maltreatment. For example, some states included "abandonment", "threats of harm to the child", and "congenital drug addiction" as "Other". The percentages total to more than 100 percent of victims because children may have been victims of more than one type of maltreatment.[4]

[4] Id

SEX AND AGE OF VICTIMS

For 2001, 48 percent of child victims were male and 51.5 percent of the victims were female. The sex for 0.5 percent of child victims was unknown or not reported.

Children in the age group of birth to 3 years accounted for 27.7 percent of victims. Overall, the rate of victimization is inversely related to the age of the child. These proportions have remained constant during the past 5 years.

VICTIMS IN RELATION TO THEIR PERPETRATORS

In order to establish whether perpetrators acted alone or in concert with others, the data were examined from the perspective of the victim. In these analyses new categories of relationship were constructed – namely, "Mother only", "Father only", "Mother and father", and other relationship combinations.

More than 10 percent (11.9%) of child victims were maltreated by a non-parental perpetrator who acted alone. Eighty-four percent of child victims were maltreated by one or more parents. Almost half of child victims (40.5%) were maltreated by a "Mother only" and a fifth of victims (19.3%) were maltreated by a "Mother and father". These percentages were similar to those in 2000[5] (Figure 5.4).

[5] Id

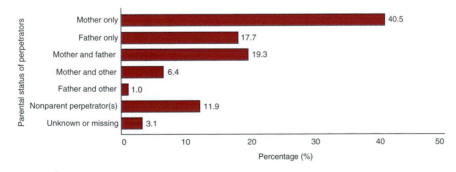

Figure 5.4[6]

[6] Id

This bar graph displays the perpetrator data from the perspective of the victim. More than 10 percent (11.9%) of victims were maltreated by a non-parental perpetrator. More than 40 percent (40.5%) of victims were maltreated by a "Mother only" and 19.3% of victims were maltreated by a "Mother and father".

PHYSICAL ABUSE

The infliction of physical injury from acts such as punching, beating, kicking, biting, burning, shaking or other harmful act.

The involvement of law enforcement in child abuse cases comes from four possible sources:

- Direct response to a scene.
- Report provided by the public-at-large.
- Report provided by health care personnel.
- Report provided by child protective services (CPS) personnel.

Note: The health practitioner in most jurisdictions is mandated to report the mere *possibility* of a child being abused. There are civil penalties incurred if reporting is not done.

NUMBER OF CHILD FATALITIES

For 2001, a national estimate of 1,300 child deaths at a rate of 1.81 children of every 100,000 children in the population died from abuse or neglect. Many states were able to supplement the automated data from the child welfare agency with statistics from other agencies in their states. Included in the reported 1,300 fatalities were 150 fatalities reported from such agencies like health departments and fatality review boards.

Deaths that occur while a child is under the custody or supervision of the child welfare agency are especially egregious. CPS in 48 states reported 18 deaths that occurred in foster care. Of these, six deaths were reported by other agencies such as the coroner's office. Approximately 1.5 percent of child fatalities reported by the states occurred in some type of out-of-home placement setting.

Child fatalities by age and sex

Fatality victims are typically very young. Children younger than 1 year accounted for 40.9 percent of fatalities and 84.5 percent were younger than 6 years of age. The risk of a child being a fatality victim declined consistently through age 4. Male children accounted for 56.0 percent and female children accounted for 44.0 percent of all fatalities.

REPORTING PARTIES IMMUNITY FROM LIABILITY

Non-sworn health professionals who report abuse cases to authorities are generally protected by state statute from personal liability. A reasonable suspicion, but *not* clear and convincing proof of abuse is required by these statutes mandating health professionals to report. Statutes require police to exercise due diligence in investigating reports of abuse.

CHILD ABUSE

Not every dental or head and neck injury on a child is from abuse. Bruising or contusions from innocent falls occur on the bony prominences of the head and face being the point of first contact. Injuries on soft tissue (non-prominent areas) are suspicious. These would be ears, top and the back of the head. Many times injuries of varying color or "age" will be present on the body. Thorough history-taking and independent interviews with both the child and custodial adults are the primary means of discerning a "clumsy" child from experiencing prolonged abusive conditions. Self-inflicted injuries are possible, from hands or teeth. Case study might include a psychological profiling if circumstances warrant suspicion of the child's story. Anatomical locations on the posterior area of the child's body generally are ruled out as being capable of self-inflicted injury (Figure 5.5).

Caveat: Differential diagnosis – Accidental injuries generally involve one side of the body. Bilateral injuries are not considered a benign injury and should be a suspect of abuse.

It is important for law enforcement officers and involved parties to consider other possibilities or medical conditions that could explain the observed conditions of a child that is suspected for abuse rather than an accidental injury.

Bruises are common in children especially connected with normal activities around the home and playground. Areas prone for most play bruises are the outside surfaces of the upper arms and the shin areas of the legs. In cases that warrant serious concern, a full panel blood test should be performed to consider medical conditions that produce excessive bruising or mimic bruising due to blood disease. The possibility of these dermatological and systemic conditions demand that complete medical survey be conducted in advance of final determinations of cause.

ELDER ABUSE

Elderly adults can be subject to severe skin aberrations mimicking injuries due to disease and side effects from anti-coagulant medicines. The elder adult may also be deficient in personal hygiene habits and experience skin sores, ulcerations and be subject to frequent bruising from falls. A custodial adult has the responsibility, however, to provide adequate care, maintenance and remedial treatment in a timely manner.

SIGNS OF ABUSE AND NEGLECT

There is never just one "stand alone" indicator of appearance or behavior that always accompanies an abused child or adult. Basic neglect of personal hygiene, apparent nutritional deficits, behavioral reluctance or reticence to interact with others, can be a part of abuse "syndromes" but are *not* indicative without corroboration with other facts.

Injury classifications

- Accidental injuries – this could be the effect of inadequate parental supervision or simply a non-culpable event.
- Intentional injuries – where the person (child or adult) is injured due to the direct actions of another person.

LOCATIONS AND TYPES OF PHYSICAL INJURIES OF ABUSED CHILDREN

HEAD AND FACE

The face, head, and the mouth are sites of over 50% of injuries in young children associated with abuse.

Caveat: Always consider multiple injuries both externally and inside the child's mouth as a possibility in every case.

The absence of hair on the head with the presence of swelling in the underlying scalp is suspect of abuse. There are, however, child behavioral disorders that result in the child impulsively pulling their hair causing scalp damage.

Under the lips are small muscles called frenums. They are easily torn by physical blows to the mouth. Forced closure of a child's mouth can produce this injury in splitting of the inner lip tissue. Some experts consider this type of injury to be a potential proof of abuse, while others disagree. There are no studies proving either opinion.

Facial bruises, contusions, scrapes, and lacerations

Head injuries from accidental causes occur during contact of the head or facial bony structures. These bony prominences are common sites of accidental injury as they are point of first contact. Bruising of the softer tissues below the cheek without accompanying bruising of the cheekbone itself is an example of suspicious injury. These would be ears, top and the back of the head as well (Figure 5.5).

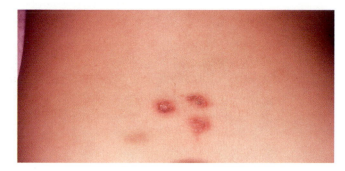

Figure 5.5

Partially healed cigarette burns on the back of a child. The differential diagnosis could be healing insect bites, but this pattern is too symmetrical with its three areas of scabbing, and the scabs are much too large.

Table 5.1

Time estimate of color changes in bruises.

Appearance	Time since occurrence
Dark red/violet	Recent
Blue/purple	1–3 days
Yellow/green	4–7 days
Light brown/tan	7–10 days

Bruising shapes and color changes over time

The healing process provides appearance changes in the outlines and color of bruises. A "rainbow effect" of multiple colors from red to tan, green and yellow may present as evidence of multiple injury episodes (Table 5.1).

OTHER LOCATIONS OF BRUISING AND WELTS SEEN IN CHILD ABUSE

- Traumatized ear lobes.
- On the neck from being choked.
- On the torso, back, buttocks, genital or thighs.

PATTERNED INJURIES

Certain objects and mechanisms that injure skin and its underlying tissue can leave outlines or shapes mimicking the object. Figure 5.6 is a clear example of this occurrence. Certain skin indentations such as bite marks can be used to create a dental profile of the biter. Injuries that are simply diffuse bruising are less valuable for identification purposes.

Ovoid marks

The presence of diffuse bite mark on arms, legs, and trunk must be evaluated as potential sign of abuse. The possibility of another sibling or playmate biting

Figure 5.6

Hand-slapping injury on a child's abdomen. The reddened outline shows that the impact actually left the inner area of each finger imprint undamaged.

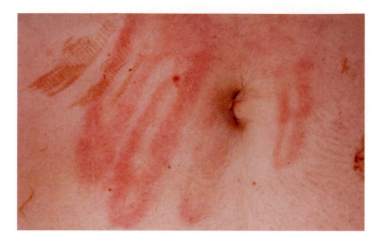

the victim is always a consideration. The relative size of the bruise can help in discerning an adult biter from a child biter. A jaw width of less than 3 cm is most likely made by another child.

Round patterns

Skin discoloration can be from:

1. Round objects such as toy wheels and similarly shaped items.
2. Discoloration from "Mongolian spots" is seen in all major racial groupings. These marks are innocuous but mimic injuries of non-accidental origin.

One-sided versus two-sided injuries

Children commonly self-injure themselves during play and daily activities. These injuries generally involve one side of the head. Bilateral injuries are not considered a benign injury.

Black eyes

Definition: Facial bruising around both eyes. Forehead injuries from an innocuous fall can produce diffuse bruising in the eye area after a passage of time (one or more days). The eyes, however, are *not* tender in this instance. Direct blows to the eyes produce tenderness in the eyelids called *raccoon eyes*.

Torso, buttocks and chest, and upper arms

Bilateral bruises of the same appearance should be considered of suspicious origin.

Parallel marks or striations

These can be tool marks from belts, buckles, electrical cords, wire coat hangers and straps (i.e. looped instruments). Also, wrist injuries can result from restraint cords.

Multiple round marks

Multiple round burns (i.e. cigarette burns) on hands and feet or eyelets of belts are definitely abusive acts. A non-abuse condition called Mongolian spots, seen on the buttocks, shoulder, backs of young children, appears as round pigmented (darkened) spots.

Burns

Burns are one of the most common injuries that occur to children from accidental means, as they start walking and climbing. These injuries are usually on the palm side of hands and forearms. A child pulling a hot liquid container onto themselves will show burns on one side of the face and torso, indicating a splash effect of the liquid. The burn will be superficial due to the rapid dissipation of the liquid as it falls off the child. Second and third degree burns with inadequate explanation should be highly suspected as abuse.

Evidence from interviews that can increase the likelihood of abuse from burns are:

1. Old burns that are not properly explained by the adult.
2. A burn pattern that is not consistent with the adult's explanation.
3. No history of how the burn occurred.
4. Delay in seeking medical treatment.

Features of child abuse burns

Immersion burns on hands and feet appear as "sock-like" or "glove-like". Burns on buttocks look like "donuts". Rope burns on arms, legs, neck or torso are created during restraining of the child. "Dry" burns are contact injuries that reflect the shape of the object (i.e. iron).

FRACTURES

Child

Small children are susceptible to falling, however, the amount of force needed for severe dental injuries and fractures require a fall from greater-than-child height and/or force beyond the typical involuntary spill.

Figure 5.7

A broken upper front tooth detected by its edge being significantly lower than adjacent teeth.

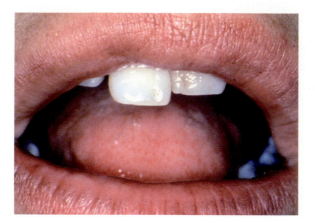

Adult

Adult assault victims will commonly show fractures of the long bones of the arm and the ribs.

Facial bone fracture injury types: adult and child

1. Skull, facial bones, mandible, maxilla, nasal bones, upper spiral fracture of arms.
2. Tooth fractures:
   – Tooth avulsions (i.e. knocked out front teeth). Pushed-in (intruded) front teeth creating breaks in the surrounding bone (Figure 5.7).
   – Loose teeth: Note, that deciduous teeth (i.e. baby teeth) become quite loose prior to falling out. Adult teeth that are loose in older children, however, are from injuries.

SIGNS OF FORCED FEEDING

Produces tears in the corners of the lips. Caustic substances can cause:

1. Burns around mouth.
2. Intraoral burns of tongue and soft palate.
3. Bruises in roof and corner of mouth.

RADIOGRAPHIC PROOF OF PREVIOUS TRAUMA

Medical head and dental X-rays can reveal broken tooth roots and other proof of previous trauma. The adult victim or child's parent should be interviewed regarding the history of old injuries of this nature.

DOCUMENTATION OF EVIDENCE

1. Note taking at the scene with use of diagrams, audio and videotaping is recommended.
2. Photographic recording:
   - 35 mm long range without a scale.
   - 35 mm color film with a scale in place. Place the scale at the same level as the piece of evidence. Place camera directly above the evidence. See Chapters 7 (The Use of Digital Imaging in Human Identification) and 9 (Photography and Forensic Dental Evidence) for examples of good and bad photography methods.
   - Avoid polaroid format for close-up and/or detailed subjects.

GLOSSARY OF ABUSE INVESTIGATION TERMS[7]

[7] Id

Adoptive parent A person with the legal relation of parent to a child not related by birth, with the same mutual rights and obligations that exist between children and their birth parents. The legal relationship has been finalized.

Age Age calculated in years at the time of the report of abuse or neglect or as of December 31 of the reporting year.

Alleged perpetrator An individual who is alleged to have caused or knowingly allowed the maltreatment of a child as stated in an incident of child abuse or neglect.

Alleged victim Child about whom a report regarding maltreatment has been made to a CPS agency.

Alternative response system A maltreatment disposition system used in some states that provides for responses other than "Substantiated", "Indicated" and "Unsubstantiated". In such a system, investigations may or may not have maltreatment victims; children may or may not be determined to be maltreatment victims. Such a system may be known as a "diversified" system or an "in need of services" system.

American Indian or Alaska Native A person having origins in any of the original peoples of North and South America (including Central America), and who maintains tribal affiliation or community attachment.

Anonymous or unknown report source An individual who reports a suspected incident of child maltreatment without identifying himself or herself; or the type of reporter is unknown.

Asian A person having origins in any of the original people of the Far East, Southeast Asia, or the Indian sub-continent, including, for example, Cambodia, China, India, Japan, Korea, Malaysia, Pakistan, the Philippine Islands, Thailand, and Vietnam.

Assessment A process by which the CPS agency determines whether the child and/or other persons involved in the report of alleged maltreatment is in need of services.

Biological parent The birth mother or father of the child rather than the adoptive or foster parent or the stepparent.

Black or African-American A person having origins in any of the black racial groups of Africa.

Caregiver A person responsible for the care and supervision of the child who was reported as an alleged victim.

Case-level data Data submitted by the states in the Child File containing individual child or report maltreatment characteristics.

Caseworker A staff person assigned to a report of child maltreatment at the time of the report disposition.

Child A person less than 18 years of age or considered to be a minor under state law.

Child day care provider A person with a temporary caregiver responsibility but who is not related to the child such as a day care center staff member, a family day care provider or a baby-sitter. Does not include persons with legal custody or guardianship of the child.

Child death review team A state team of professionals who reviews all reports surrounding the death of a child.

Child Protective Services (CPS) An official agency of a state having the responsibility for CPS and activities.

CPS supervisor The manager of the caseworker assigned to a report of child maltreatment at the time of the report disposition.

CPS worker The person assigned to a report of child maltreatment at the time of the report disposition.

CPS workforce The CPS supervisors and workers assigned to handle a child maltreatment report. May include other administrative staff as defined by the state agency table of organization.

Child record A case-level record in the Child File containing the data associated with one child in one given report.

Child victim A child for whom an incident of abuse or neglect has been substantiated or indicated by an investigation or assessment. A state may include some children with alternative dispositions as victims.

Child's living arrangement The home environment, i.e.: family or substitute care, in which the child was residing at the time of the report.

Children's bureau Federal agency within the Administration on Children, Youth and Families, Administration for Children and Families, U.S. Department of Health and Human Services, which is responsible for the collection and analysis of National Child Abuse and Neglect Data System (NCANDS) data.

Closed with no finding Disposition that does not conclude with a specific finding because the investigation could not be completed for such reasons as: the family moved out of the jurisdiction, the family could not be located or necessary diagnostic or other reports were not received within required time limits.

Court-appointed representative A person appointed by the court to represent a child in a neglect or abuse proceeding. May be an attorney or a court-appointed special advocate (or both) and is often referred to as a guardian ad litem. The representative makes recommendations to the court concerning the best interests of the child.

Court-appointed special advocate Adult volunteers trained to advocate for abused and neglected children involved in the juvenile court.

Court action Legal action initiated by a representative of the CPS agency on behalf of the child. This includes authorization to place the child, filing for temporary custody, dependency or termination of parental rights. It does not include criminal proceedings against a perpetrator.

Education personnel Employees of a public, private educational institution or program; includes teachers, teacher assistants, administrators and others directly associated with the delivery of educational services.

Family preservation services Activities designed to protect children from harm and to assist families at risk or in crisis, including services to prevent placement, to support the reunification of children with their families or to support the continued placement of children in adoptive homes or other permanent living arrangements.

Family support services Community-based preventive activities designed to alleviate stress and promote parental competencies and behaviors that will increase the ability of families to nurture their children successfully, enable families to use other resources and opportunities available in the community and create supportive networks to enhance childrearing abilities of parents.

Fatality Death of a child as a result of abuse or neglect, because either (a) an injury resulting from the abuse or neglect was the cause of death or (b) abuse and/or neglect were contributing factors to the cause of death.

Foster care Twenty-four hour substitute care for children placed away from their parents or guardians and for whom the state agency has placement and care responsibility. This includes family foster homes, foster homes of relatives, group homes, emergency shelters, residential facilities, child care institutions and pre-adoptive homes regardless of whether the facility is licensed and whether payments are made by the state or local agency for the care of the child, or whether there is Federal matching of any payments made. Foster care may be provided by those related or not related to the child. All children in care for more than 24 hours are counted.

Foster parent An individual licensed to provide a home for orphaned, abused, neglected, delinquent or disabled children, usually with the approval of the government or a social service agency. May be a relative or a non-relative.

Friend A non-relative acquainted with the child, the parent, or caregiver including landlords, clergy or youth group workers (e.g., Scouts, Little League coaches).

Group home or residential care A non-familial 24-hour care facility which may be supervised by the state agency or governed privately.

Hispanic or Latino ethnicity A person of Cuban, Mexican, Puerto Rican, South or Central American, or other Spanish culture or origin regardless of race.

Indicated or reason to suspect An investigation disposition that concludes that maltreatment cannot be substantiated under state law or policy, but there is reason to suspect that the child may have been maltreated or was at risk of maltreatment. This is applicable only to states that distinguish between "Substantiated" and "Indicated" dispositions.

Initial investigation The CPS initial contact or attempt to have face-to-face contact with the alleged victim. If face-to-face contact is not possible with the alleged victim, initial investigation would be when CPS first contacted any party who could provide information essential to the investigation or assessment.

Intake The activities associated with the receipt of a referral, the assessment or screening, the decision to accept and the enrollment of individuals or families into services.

Intentionally false "Unsubstantiated" investigation disposition about which it has been concluded that the person reporting the alleged incident of maltreatment knew that the allegation was not true.

Investigation The gathering and assessment of objective information to determine if a child has been or is at risk of being maltreated. Generally includes face-to-face contact with the victim and results in a disposition as to whether the alleged report is substantiated or not.

Investigation disposition A determination made by a social service agency that evidence is or is not sufficient under state law to conclude that maltreatment occurred.

Investigation disposition date The point in time at the end of the investigation/assessment when a CPS worker declares a disposition to the child maltreatment report.

Investigation start date The date when CPS initially contacted or attempted to have face-to-face contact with the alleged victim. If this face-to-face contact is not possible, the date would be when CPS initially contacted any party who could provide information essential to the investigation or assessment.

Juvenile court petition A legal document filed with the court of original jurisdiction overseeing matters affecting children. The petition typically requests that the court take action regarding the child's status as a result of an investigation. Usually, a petition requests that the child be declared a dependent or delinquent child, or that the child be placed in an out-of-home setting.

Legal guardian Adult person who has been given legal custody and guardianship of a minor.

Legal, law enforcement, or criminal justice personnel People employed by a local, state, tribal or Federal justice agency including law enforcement, courts, district attorney's office, probation or other community corrections agency, and correctional facilities.

Maltreatment An act or failure to act by a parent, caregiver or other person as defined under state law which results in physical abuse, neglect, medical neglect, sexual abuse, emotional abuse or an act or failure to act which presents an imminent risk of serious harm to a child.

Maltreatment type A particular form of child maltreatment determined by investigation to be substantiated or indicated under state law. Types include physical abuse, neglect or deprivation of necessities, medical neglect, sexual abuse, psychological or emotional maltreatment and other forms included in state law.

Medical neglect A type of maltreatment caused by failure by the caregiver to provide for the appropriate health care of the child although financially able to do so, or offered financial or other means to do so.

Medical personnel People employed by a medical facility or practice including physicians, physician assistants, nurses, emergency medical technicians, dentists, chiropractors, coroners and dental assistants and technicians.

Mental health personnel People employed by a mental health facility or practice including psychologists, psychiatrists, therapists, etc.

Native Hawaiian or other Pacific Islander A person having origins in any of the original peoples of Hawaii, Guam, Samoa or other Pacific Islands.

NCANDS The National Child Abuse and Neglect Data System.

Neglect or deprivation of necessities A type of maltreatment that refers to the failure by the caregiver to provide needed, age-appropriate care although financially able to do so or offered financial or other means to do so.

Neighbor A person living in close geographical proximity to the child or family.

Non-caregiver A person who is not responsible for the care and supervision of the child including school personnel, friends and neighbors.

Non-parent Includes other relative, foster parent, residential facility staff, child day care provider, substitute care provider, unmarried partner of parent, legal guardian and other.

Not substantiated Investigation disposition that determines that there is not sufficient evidence under state law or policy to conclude that the child has been maltreated or is at risk of being maltreated.

Out-of-court contact Contact, which is not part of the actual judicial hearing, between the court-appointed representative and the child victim. Such contacts enable the court-appointed representative to obtain a first-hand understanding of the situation and needs of the child victim and to make recommendations to the court concerning the best interests of the child.

Parent The birth mother/father, adoptive mother/father, or stepmother/father of the child.

Perpetrator The person who has been determined to have caused or knowingly allowed the maltreatment of the child.

Perpetrator age at report Age of an individual determined to have caused or knowingly allowed the maltreatment of a child. Age is calculated in years at the time of the report of child maltreatment.

Perpetrator relationship Primary role of the perpetrator with a child victim of maltreatment.

Physical abuse Type of maltreatment that refers to physical acts that caused or could have caused physical injury to the child.

Prior victim A child victim with previous substantiated or indicated incidents of maltreatment.

Psychological or emotional maltreatment Type of maltreatment that refers to acts or omissions other than physical abuse or sexual abuse, that caused or could have caused, conduct, cognitive, affective or other mental disorders. Includes emotional neglect, psychological abuse, mental injury. Frequently occurs as verbal abuse or excessive demands on a child's performance.

Receipt of report The log-in of a call to the agency from a reporter alleging child maltreatment.

Relative A person connected to the child by blood, such as parents, siblings, grandparents.

Removal date The month, day and year that the child was removed from the care and supervision of parents or parental substitutes, during or as a result of an investigation by the CPS or social services agency. If a child has been removed more than once, the removal date is the first removal in concert with the investigation.

Report Notification to the CPS agency of suspected child maltreatment. This can include one or more children.

Report date The month, day and year that the responsible agency was notified of the suspected child maltreatment.

Report disposition The conclusion reached by the responsible agency regarding the report of maltreatment pertaining to the child.

Report disposition date The month, day and year that a decision was made by the CPS agency or court regarding the disposition of a report or investigation of alleged child maltreatment.

Report identifier A unique identification assigned to each report of child maltreatment for the purposes of the NCANDS data collection.

Report source The category or role of the person who makes a report of alleged maltreatment.

Reporting period The 12-month period for which data are submitted to the NCANDS. The calendar year is requested.

Residential facility staff Employees of a public or private group residential facility, including emergency shelters, group homes and institutions.

Response time with respect to the initial investigation The time between the log-in of a call to the state agency from a reporter alleging child maltreatment and the face-to-face contact with the alleged victim, where this is appropriate or to contact with another person who can provide information.

Response time with respect to the provision of services The time from the log-in of a call to the agency from a reporter alleging child maltreatment to the provision of post-investigative services; often requiring the opening of a case for ongoing services.

Screened-in reports Reports that met the state's standards for accepting a child maltreatment report.

Screened-out reports Reports that did not meet the state's standards for accepting a child maltreatment report.

Screening The process of making a decision about whether or not to accept a report to the state agency which receives child maltreatment reports.

Services Non-investigative public or private non-profit activities provided or continued as a result of an investigation or assessment. In general, only activities that occur within 90 days of the report are included in NCANDS.

Sexual abuse A type of maltreatment that refers to the involvement of the child in sexual activity to provide sexual gratification or financial benefit to the perpetrator, including contacts for sexual purposes, molestation, statutory rape, prostitution, pornography, exposure, incest or other sexually exploitative activities.

Social services block grant Funds provided by title XX of the Social Security Act that are used for services to the states that may include child care, child protection, child and foster care services and day care.

Social services personnel Employees of a public or private social services or social welfare agency or other social worker or counselor who provides similar services.

State agency The agency in a state that is responsible for child protection and child welfare.

Stepparent The husband or wife, by a subsequent marriage, of the child's mother or father.

Substantiated A type of investigation disposition that concludes that the allegation of maltreatment or risk of maltreatment was supported or founded by state law or state policy. This is the highest level of finding by a state agency.

Substitute care provider A person providing out-of-home care to children such as a foster parent or residential facility staff.

Unable to determine Any racial category not included in the following: American Indian or Alaska Native, Asian, Black or African-American, Native Hawaiian or Other Pacific Islander or White.

Unknown The state collects data on this variable, but the data for this particular report or child were not captured or are missing.

Unmarried partner of parent Someone who has a relationship with the parent and lives in the household with the parent and abused child.

Unsubstantiated A type of investigation disposition that determines that there is not sufficient evidence under state law to conclude or suspect that the child has been maltreated or is at risk of being maltreated.

Victim A child having a maltreatment disposition of "Substantiated", "Indicated" or "Alternative Response Victim".

White A person having origins in any of the original peoples of Europe, the Middle East or North African.

CHAPTER 6

DENTAL INVESTIGATIONS IN MASS DISASTER INCIDENTS

OVERVIEW

Law enforcement is asked to be in charge of the integrity of airline crashes, terrorist attacks and natural disaster scenes. They often are involved in the actual recovery of human remains. Preparation of sworn personnel in the basic organizational requirements for such conditions is mandatory. This chapter gives the forensic framework surrounding *mass fatality incidents* (MFI) where law enforcement performs a vital link in the chain of human identification efforts.

A single unknown body requiring identification can easily be handled in any medical examiner/coroner's office (MEC). A *mass disaster* occurs when numbers exceed the capacity of the local jurisdiction responsible for forensic investigation. When a situation such as a commercial aircraft mishap occurs, the situation changes dramatically. The 2001 terrorist attacks at the World Trade Center, Pentagon, and Pennsylvania, USA have become prototype scenarios of this kind of unexpected tragedy (Figure 6.1).

Figure 6.1

Commercial aircraft fragments from a high-speed impact that did not involve post-crash fire. It is common for human remains to be present in the tangled pieces of aircraft.

Forensic Dental Evidence
ISBN: 0-1212-1042-1

The *rescue* of survivors is the initial response undertaken by fire, police and EMS agencies. The *recovery* of human remains is phased into the response team effort as time and circumstances progress. The need to identify hundreds or thousands of victims takes time, coordination and dedication. The existence of a *disaster contingency plan* is crucial to the proper handling of this type of situation although each event has its own unforeseen challenges. Jurisdictional overlaps range from local, state and federal to individual branches of the military. The Armed Forces Institute of Pathology (AFIP), the Armed Forces Medical Examiner or the Department of Defense, FBI, FAA, Interpol or an international equivalent may play a role. In international travel situations, the US State department may be involved if US citizens are killed or missing.

DENTAL RESPONSE

Large cities or counties may have their own dental identification teams. State and national dental associations may sponsor teams as well. Members of identification teams typically include anthropologists, pathologists and radiologists as well as dentists. Fingerprint specialists from the FBI, Interpol or other law enforcement agencies are also important contributors to the identification process. Personal effects, fingerprints and dental comparisons generally account for the majority of positive identifications.

FACILITIES FOR MASS DISASTER IDENTIFICATION

A *temporary morgue* will be established if the disaster overwhelms the local facilities of the MEC. A hangar at an airport or a large warehouse is a frequently chosen site (Figures 6.2 and 6.3). A concrete floor is always preferable to wood for health and safety reasons. Location of the site will be impacted by several factors. The distance of the actual recovery site to the morgue will have a bearing on the length of time necessary for the identification of the victims. Deep-sea recoveries are more complicated and time consuming than most land-based operations. Matters of logistics and safety must not be ignored as family, media and community leaders expect identifications.

PROCESSING HUMAN REMAINS

If practical, a land-based body recovery site should be organized into a grid system. This establishes fixed points of reference as wreckage and remains are recovered. This allows later association of fragments recovered, reconstruction of identities and events that took place. An aerial view of the scene with grid in place may also be helpful. If practical, photographs of human remains (HR)

Figure 6.2

Temporary morgue setup in a warehouse. The partitions separate the various forensic disciplines as each case is transported via gurney. The dental section consists of a portable X-ray and developing machine, computer terminals and data software programs, disposable supplies, light boxes, and hard copy documents.

Figure 6.3

The placement of refrigeration trucks immediately adjacent to the temporary morgue requires added measures for visual and perimeter security.

should be taken *before* removal. Knowing certain victims in are from a specific location can aid in identifying associated evidence. Airline manifests and seating plans will be made available to the forensic team and are used to gain access to antemortem dental/medical records. Human remains may be intact but may also be highly fragmented, burned, crushed or completely destroyed. All HR not physically attached should be contained in separately labeled body bags or containers. *Accession* and inventory control are important to achieve an organized and complete result. The use of bar code labels will allow for

Figure 6.4

Typical example of dental remains (intact jaw) that are barely attached to a torso. The chances of individual teeth being dislodged during a high-energy impact are quite high. In a land-based recovery site, this may require sifting through ash and debris to recover small dental fragments.

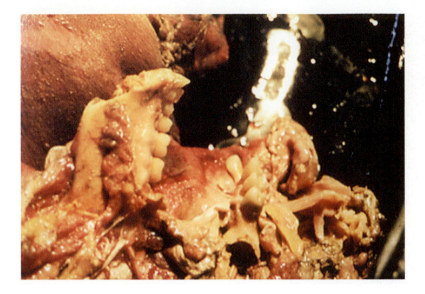

automated computer input of information in incidents with a high number of fragments.

The mere proximity of one body part to another does not indicate that they came from the same individual. Indeed, the unintentional commingling of remains can result in great confusion. There will be significant extra expenditure of time in discovering (hopefully) and correcting the resultant problems. Prevention of commingling of multiple persons' body parts starts with careful removal at the scene. Heads should be bagged to eliminate loose teeth from falling out and being lost. Personnel at the recovery site are tasked with a crucial role. Knowledgeable, trained people should serve and manage in these capacities, where the recognition of human material is paramount and knowledge of human identification processing is mandatory (Figure 6.4).

The formulation of a disaster management plan in advance of an actual incident is necessary to achieve a modicum of organizational wisdom rather than mere reaction when a disaster occurs. The disaster plan should be reviewed regularly, with key agencies updating contact information, facility requirements and confirming agreements with outside suppliers and support personnel. In the case of elected coroners and sheriffs and new agency appointees, continuity needs to be maintained with prior efforts in disaster planning.

IDENTIFICATION METHODS

A typical disaster morgue operation will include stations for photography, personal effects, fingerprints, radiology, dental, anthropology, pathology and DNA sampling for later laboratory analysis (Figure 6.5). Mortuary processing,

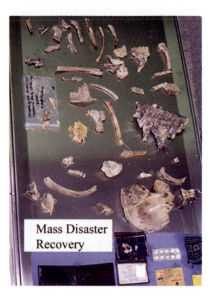

Figure 6.5

This combination of human, non-human remains and personal effects were recovered from the ocean bottom at an average depth of 700 feet.

storage and shipping will take place once all necessary operations have been completed and identifications have been reviewed and triple checked. Thorough documentation will continue along the entire route of this process.

Personal effects

In some cases, the personal effects will include jewelry of considerable value. All items should be carefully safeguarded. Inscriptions will be quite helpful. A catalog of items should be created in order to facilitate the return of personal effects. This includes items that have been packed in suitcases and transported in the cargo hold. These may be very important to the families and represent a final connection to their loved one.

Clothing on body fragments provides important information in the *association* of separately recovered body parts during the later stages in the identification process. Since fragments are not recovered simultaneously in the field, the commonality of underwear and outer clothing remnants still attached saves the tremendous cost of DNA processing of multiple body fragments.

Fingerprints

Fingerprint analysis can usually be accomplished, unless fire, decomposition or other postmortem actions have destroyed the soft tissue on fingers. Depending on the age and past history of the victim there may or may not be fingerprint records on file. A victim's history of military service, government or private employment requiring security clearance could lead to old records.

The younger adult populations, however, have a lower percentage of archived fingerprints.

X-Ray examination of HR

Full-length radiographs should be taken through the body bags. Occasionally, stray dental fragments and personal effects are discovered imbedded in soft tissue. In the case of military or terrorist action, explosives may also be found. Evidence of past trauma or surgery may be seen. A hip replacement, spinal fusion, healed fracture, pin or wire placement, old shrapnel wounds or other unusual findings can be very helpful when compared with medical history records.

Precautions must be in place for the protection of recovery and morgue personnel, such as lead shielding and monitoring badges. All occupational safety and health administration (OSHA) standards must be upheld to avoid mechanical, biological or chemical injury to workers.

Anthropology

The anthropology section is helpful in cases where incineration and dismemberment have created multiple body parts that are unidentifiable. The anthropologists initially attempt to sort the human material according to sex and age. The possible identification of a bony fragment as a skull belonging to a man or woman or possessing certain racial trait or belonging to an age range can narrow the field of possible identifications from a passenger manifest or missing persons list.

Dental processing

Once the human dental remains arrive at the morgue's dental area they will be photographed. After this step, the pathology section generally resects jaws from the unviewable remains to allow visualization and radiographic examination. Full mouth dental radiographs will be taken. The presence of an automatic X-ray processor is quite helpful. Once the dry films are mounted they can be evaluated for quality, appropriate angulation and the possible need to retake some views. If that determination is not made at this point, bringing the body back from further down the line becomes a major challenge. Good quality films are extremely important as objective evidence.

Postmortem dental profiling

One person should perform the postmortem oral examination, while another looks on confirming the findings and a third recording the findings on proper dental charts. This data may then be entered by the team into a computer program to collate and cross-reference information. Double-checking is vital in order to be absolutely accurate. The chart that results from the unknown victim will be used as a comparison with all available antemortem records.

Antemortem dental record profiling

Compiling antemortem records takes place as the field recovery of remains is ongoing. Family members are contacted for the names of treating dentists, who in turn are requested to forward all original records for the individual in question. Such records will include narratives, graphics, radiographs, photographs, laboratory prescriptions, referral notes and anything else that has been generated through the course of treatment. The antemortem team will have the task of deciphering illegible handwriting, making sense of codes and abbreviations, translating foreign languages and interpreting notations. They will follow up with the originating dentist, if necessary, for clarification and confirmation. This step can be a painstaking task when numbers of missing persons are large. Computer assisted identification through the use of the WINID software program (www.winid.com) allows organization of data and X-rays necessary for investigation.

Comparison of antemortem and postmortem dental profiles

Once the records of a particular individual's antemortem records are studied, all findings are recorded on a single document form which is identical to the one being used by the postmortem examination team. This facilitates the comparison phase of the process. If, for instance, tooth number three has had a root canal treatment and crown, that feature can be looked for specifically eliminating the cases where this combination is not present. If a set of remains does not include the maxilla or if tooth number three has been lost due to the trauma of the event, this point of comparison will not be applicable. Those remains cannot be eliminated yet and other points will have to be compared.

Frequently, there will be minor inconsistencies in the ante- and postmortem radiographs. They will usually be related to the passage of time and additional treatment being rendered. The ever-present possibility of human error always exists, as well. As long as these small differences can be explained they do not present a problem. The presence of a single irreconcilable discrepancy will preclude a positive identification. Examples would be the presence of a tooth postmortem when the tooth was absent antemortem or the presence of a virgin tooth subsequent to the placement of restorative material. The number or shape of roots is a feature that would not change and an inconsistency of this type would also eliminate the possibility of identification with that set of antemortem records.

Digital comparison of these various radiographs insures dental anatomical, restorative and dimensional relationships can be studied accurately and electronically recorded for future presentation to families and judicial review.

Obviously, all efforts should be made to avoid errors in the final disposition of the remains. An incorrect identification with subsequent release of the remains to the storage facility or the incorrect family will create a double problem. The correct body will remain unidentified due to the mistake and a family will be further traumatized.

CHALLENGES IN MASS DISASTER MANAGEMENT

Large numbers of victims create a challenging environment for the forensic odontologist. Due to high g-force and speed impacts, explosions and crushing, there can be tremendous destruction resulting in fragmentation, commingling and burning. Commercial flight manifests may be inaccurate. People may be traveling under false names and certain modes of transportation do not require positive identification for ticketing. Establishing who is expected to be among the victims becomes difficult in locations where there are large populations of people. It took months for authorities in New York to create an accurate count of victims.

COMMUNICATION

The sharing of information between different sections of the forensic identification center is crucial for a successful conclusion of the operation. The recovery teams may also benefit with communication from the identification team. Internal communication within the identification facility is also vital. For instance, the antemortem dental team may discover a surgical procedure noted on a medical history form. They can then alert the pathology section to be on the lookout. Much time is wasted on incomplete investigation when there is lack of cross-referencing medical information. Less than accurate and incomplete information will degrade the ultimate results.

The dental comparison process is seriously jeopardized if treating dentists cannot be located or records and radiographs are poor or missing. Occasionally, issues related to politics, jurisdiction or legalities will complicate a situation. A constant effort needs to be made by all agencies responding to an MFI to foster positive working relationships and agreements on protocols. Flexibility and adaptation to problems are important concepts. Things never stay static for very long during an MFI.

FAMILY ASSISTANCE CENTER

Professionally trained staff at a centralized meeting location in a major hotel or community center should assist families and friends over their loss. The purpose is two-fold: humanitarian support for the families, and to facilitate obtaining vital identification information and DNA reference samples from the victims' relatives.

COUNSELING ASSISTANCE DURING AND AFTER AN MFI

The stress and strain of providing identification services in mass disasters creates health concerns for both staff and volunteers. Ongoing psychological assessment of working conditions and individuals must be an integral part of the system. Coping skills and healthy discussion of personal issues must be emphasized and fostered during and after an MFI response.

SCENARIO OF A 100-PASSENGER COMMERCIAL AIRLINE ACCIDENT

All passengers and crew died in the crash in the ocean some 8 miles off the California coast. All had extensive disfiguring injuries. All but a few of the bodies were fragmented. Eighty-five of the 88 victims were eventually identified. No inconsistencies with the manifest provided by XYZ Airlines were found. Sixty-two of the 85 identified persons (73%) were initially identified by conventional identification means. Roughly, dental comparisons, fingerprints, tattoos and personal effects identified equal numbers of crash victims conventionally. The other 23 victims were identified by paternity-type DNA testing. The 26 victims not initially identified by conventional means had court-ordered death certificates issued by petition of the MEC 6 weeks after the crash. Twenty-three of those were amended later when DNA results physically established death. Many fragments of the bodies were identified and "re-associated" with conventionally identified remains by comparison to the DNA extracted from biopsies of the conventionally identified remains.

In total, approximately 1,000 pieces of HR were recovered, representing about 60% of the estimated weight of the victims. In the initial 3 days following the crash, approximately 300 pieces of HR, representing more than half the weight of the recovered remains, were collected from the surface of the ocean by fishermen, Coast Guard, local county staff, other private boaters and US Navy personnel. Approximately 300 pieces of HR were recovered by Navy staff using remote-controlled submarines from the "debris field" on the ocean floor at a depth of about 700 feet. The remaining recovered HR was collected in fishing nets dragged through the debris field. The recovery lasted 6 weeks. The temporary morgue was closed after 4 weeks. No HR ever washed to the shore 10 miles away. Conventional identification was essentially completed within 6 weeks of the crash; most within the first several weeks. The Department of Health and Human Services – Disaster Mortuary Response Team (DMORT) helped with this process, staffing the temporary morgue at a local military base. DNA testing and identification was completed 10 months after the crash. About 280 small specimens of HR tissue, weighing in aggregate about 30 pounds, were not identified and were buried as unidentified remains. The Armed Forces DNA Identification Laboratory (AFDIL) final DNA report was received 14 months after the crash. It indicated 135 biopsies were not identifiable by DNA.

A private provider was hired by XYZ Airline to handle the identification, preparation and return of personal property.

The reader should be mindful that some of the comments and suggestions below are specific for relatively high-speed crashes into water, such as the XYZ Airline crash.

In the XYZ crash the airplane and the great majority of bodies were fragmented and scattered on the surface of the water and on the ocean floor. In such situations, documenting the exact location of where the remains were recovered is obviously of no value in helping to establish identification.

MFI RECOMMENDATIONS

1. THE LOCAL MEC NEEDS FOR IMMEDIATE INFORMATION

A disaster protocol for an MFI may be in place when an event occurs. Unfortunately, pre-planning cannot predict what specifically may be required. There will be a tremendous amount of information gathering done by the local jurisdiction and MEC at the time of an event, regardless of any preparation done in advance.

The overseeing governmental agency (state or federal) in charge of emergency response in a mass disaster should fax or courier a brief guide explaining the various assistance options to the MEC within hours of the incident. In the US this should include mention of the services available through the AFIP (US Army), the FBI and DHHS-DMORT (available on request). Providing information about the Federal Family Assistance Plan for Aviation Disasters would be helpful. This guide could also suggest the following strategies for the MEC to follow during the initial collection and storage of HR recovered from an MFI.

Inventory control

The guide should include suggestions about simple numbering of HR specimens when identification will be a problem due to expected high fragmentation or poor condition of remains.

Triage of recovered remains

Separation of HR into categories of increasingly difficult conventional (non-DNA) identification:

Probably identifiable

Larger body segments with teeth for dental record comparison, hands for printing, tattoos, unique personal effects clearly attached to the body or other obvious individual features (Figure 6.6).

Possibly identifiable

Larger body parts without obvious potentially identifiable features.

Probably not identifiable

The majority of tissue collected in a crash like the XYZ Airlines crash – small pieces of soft tissue and bone.

DNA collection protocols

Prompt biopsy of HR for future DNA testing should be integral to the initial forensic processing. The AFDIL, in Rockville, Maryland, USA, standardizes these methods at the time of this writing.

Figure 6.6

These human remains are considered "probably identifiable". In large mass disasters, the initial sorting of remains into the various difficulty levels of "identity" gives the MEC information regarding what resources will be needed for the effort.

Limitations of DNA testing

DNA testing is neither always possible, nor always conclusive. It is expensive and time consuming. Decisions on what biological specimens to collect from the total recovered HR directly affects the cost and duration of the investigation. For example, taking samples and profiling specimens from remains already identified increases workload, cost and the time-line of the recovery. Storage of these same remains is extended for months until the DNA work is completed. Most families want identification done expeditiously and want identified HR released to them for burial or cremation.

2.   MEDIA AND PUBLIC INFORMATION RESPONSE

Public information is a primary service and responsibility of the MEC and certain responding agencies. Close coordination is required between the MEC and the public information officers of all these agencies. The length of time the public needs information far exceeds the physical recovery phase of most mass disasters. Quite often airlines involved take a pro-active role in this aspect. The MEC however remains the repository of answers to vital questions concerning status of identification, recovery plans, disposition of remains and any prolonged investigation due to the disaster's circumstances.

3.   CUSTODIAL RESPONSIBILITIES FOR RECORDS AND FAMILY CONTACT

This task may involve multiple agencies that start coordinated but experience discontinuity over a long response period due to staff departures and "closing down". The families are not aware or concerned with administrative challenges. Plans must be made to continue a centralized source of data entry, record keeping, updating, control and management throughout the entire incident. As conventional identification progresses, families ask legitimate questions about the condition of the remains that were identified and ready for release. Answering those questions is a routine function of MEC offices. However, the multi-agency layering that originally gets setup to assist families may dissipate over time. Difficult investigations needing DNA profiling may not obtain results for months or possibly years with the only remaining local contact for families being the MEC.

   The problems with handling an airline disaster are far from over when the immediate Family Assistance Center closes. DNA related issues have greatly increased and prolonged the identification and HR handling workload. Most MEC offices will need continuing support beyond the initial days of HR recovery and conventional identification.

4. THE MANY ROADS TO "POSITIVE IDENTIFICATION"

Management and scientific professional staff should develop a pragmatic understanding of the many valid ways postmortem human identification can be made. The totality of the circumstances must be considered in human identification and the importance of personal effects, such as unique jewelry, clothing and wallets. Even tattoos are important factors. Personal effects and tattoos should be actively documented and pursued as tools to help establish identification, just as dental examinations, fingerprints and unique old bony defects are used. This flight had a population of only 88 individuals to choose from. In such a situation a particular tattoo or a particular ring becomes very specific. The protracted and expensive process of DNA identification should not be used to delay or discount conventional identification methodology. The MEC ultimately takes the responsibility to decide when recovered HR are sufficiently identified.

Efforts of the entire ID staff should be directed to the "probable" first then the "possible", rather than processing each specimen blindly as it is taken out of the refrigerated storage truck. This assures the obviously identifiable bodies are examined and identified for release as soon as practical.

5. QUALITY CONTROL ISSUES REGARDING DNA BIOPSY METHODS

Biopsies of HR for DNA should be taken early as possible, perhaps during the initial inventory, to minimize decomposition and degradation of the samples. A freezer for DNA biopsy storage should be part of any mass disaster morgue.

Mislabeling of specimens will occur due to human error. A numbering system should be simple and be used throughout the entire event. Bar code labeling should be encouraged.

Commingling of HR occurs in accidents and events where large numbers of people are killed in a group. The only way to handle events of this type is to individually bag each piece of HR. In this disaster, when DNA test results began arriving at the MEC office, it became apparent that some of the DNA biopsies had been mislabeled (by hand) or commingled tissue had been biopsied or that inadequate biopsy technique or improper biopsy handling had led to inconclusive test results. The MEC installed improved methods in handling later HR specimens that resulted in virtually all of those biopsies yielding positive DNA results. This suggests that more training or more care in the DNA biopsy process is warranted.

6. COMPUTER OPERATIONS RELATING TO FORENSIC IDENTIFICATION

Computer operations devoted to assisting the recording of medical/dental/personal information consumes much manpower and time for its utility in helping make identifications. In the XYZ crash, only one of the 62 conventional identifications was made with the aid of the computer. That identification was by means of a tattoo. Larger MFI certainly require extensive computer assistance. Assigning an individual to the duty of visually comparing found tattoos, unique jewelry, etc. with antemortem descriptions of identifying features collected from family interviews are suggested.

Any computer data must not be considered a "sure fix" for multi-fatality events. Individuals tasked to receive, record and collate this information must thoroughly understand how identification is processed. The communication of any computer data findings to the identification section must be done on a regular, updated basis.

7. DOCUMENTATION ACCURACY

Paper files left with the MEC by departing agencies are often in disarray. Many contain incomplete reports and rough draft reports, blank forms and incomplete forms, misfiled forms, reports and photos and mislabeled photos. As DNA results come back months after federal agencies left, the task of insuring that the file description for an HR specimen identified by DNA as a particular individual actually fit will be more difficult because of file disorder. Additionally, as attorneys request the file documentation of injuries and identification of decedents for the civil legal proceedings stemming from the incident, file disarray increases the chance of accusations of errors. Since legal actions are the rule rather than the exception in mass fatalities, it is mandatory to insure a proper chain of custody of all reports, photographs and specimens.

8. DECISIONS TO RECOVER AND WHEN TO STOP THE RECOVERY?

Sensitive issues that came up during the XYZ crash recovery centered around how extensive the search for HR should be and where to draw the line on recovering very small pieces of tissue. These issues are obviously emotionally and politically sensitive but should not be ignored and should not be deferred to the local medical examiner.

In the XYZ crash, efforts to recover remains from 700 feet below the ocean surface lasted over a month in potentially dangerous seas. The yield was diminishing as the weeks went on. Eventually the search was terminated, but not until after robotic submarine search of the airplane wreckage debris field and dragging fishing nets along the ocean floor in the area of the debris field. Despite these efforts, no traces of three crash victims and only about 60% of the total body mass of the victims were recovered. This is not surprising, given ocean currents and ocean predators. Questions must be asked regarding policy involving how much effort, how much risk to life and how much money should go into recovering the obviously fragmented remains of already known victims who are already "buried at sea". People could have died trying to recover remains from the XYZ crash. Some families asked why remains could not just have been left at sea. The disposition of small fragments of DNA identified tissue months after the initial incident was resisted by many families and resented by a few. It is certainly debatable whether returning a small test tube of tissue to a family would give them any satisfaction, especially when it has been many months after the crash. The family already knows their loved one died in the crash. They already have received a valid death certificate and financial affairs have been settled.

Terminating a search for more HR could be justified when enough remains have been observed or collected to establish a reasonable likelihood that all occupants died in the crash and when there is no reason to believe that the airplane manifest might be inaccurate. Obviously, degree of difficulty or danger in accessing the remains should influence policy about collection.

The DNA testing should follow the same pattern: testing the conventionally identified HR biopsies and the larger HR biopsies first. This would increase efficiency by yielding more new DNA patterns earlier, since there is a greater chance that large pieces of HR are from different individuals than tiny pieces of HR. This would increase the chance that not all recovered HR DNA samples need be tested, since DNA from all individuals known to be on board might be obtained before all the small fragments are tested.

CHAPTER 7

THE USE OF DIGITAL IMAGING IN HUMAN IDENTIFICATION*

Law enforcement and related investigators should have an understanding of digital imaging methods utilized by forensic dentists and others who use similar methods to analyze physical evidence. This chapter outlines these methods and gives the reader an overview on this subject. While this chapter is moderately advanced and geared primarily for mid-level to advanced imaging technicians, it will give crime scene examiners and law enforcement an idea of some of the capabilities in the realm of digital imaging methods.

Forensic dentists form their opinions on the basis of direct superimposition of questioned (Q, a bite mark or postmortem X-ray) and a known sample (K, a suspect's teeth or antemortem dental X-ray). Courts allow experts to present photographs of physical evidence (exemplars) in court that have sufficient identification value to demonstrate features that support the expert's opinion on the case. Hence, photographic accuracy and dimensional control of images are very important, demanding rigorous attention to scale dimensions and the detection of photographic distortion. Dental comparison techniques used are similar to the physical comparison of Q and K evidence in fingerprint, ballistics and tool mark studies. These disciplines have the criminalist using a comparison microscope to place the Q and K evidence samples side by side. The loops, whorls, striations, indentations, accidental (shape changes from use and aging) and class (general features of a large group of similar objects) characteristics present in the evidence samples may then be visually compared. What are difficult to assess, both in the crime and dental lab, are the dimensional values (height and width) of the evidence samples. In forensic dentistry, the traditional ruler and protractor measurements and shape comparison processes are manually derived from evidence photographs and plaster models of a suspect's teeth. These methods vary between examiners and are not accurate to greater than ±0.1 cm. Digital measurements by multiple examiners have been tested to within ±0.05 cm accuracy during numerous training sessions. Alternatively, some crime lab analysts and dentists ignore size comparisons and focus on

* Material in this chapter derived from *Digital Analysis of Bite Mark Evidence*, Johansen RJ, Bowers CM, Copyright 2003, Forensic Imaging Services, Santa Barbara, CA

similarities in class and individual features. In both situations, the possibility of error arises from examiner-subjective methods and partial selection of the available physical information. Two-dimensional digital measurement of distances and angulations are quite easily accomplished, via a desktop computer and high quality computer monitor and should lend itself to determinations of similarities/dissimilarities of physical evidences.

The recent development of digital imaging software and imaging devices such as scanners and digital cameras has created an opportunity to better control some well-recognized photographic variables and allows the forensic examiner to turn the computer monitor into a comparison microscope with the added benefit of the following functions:

- Accurate means of measuring physical parameters of crime scene evidence.
- Correction of common photographic distortion and size discrepancies.
- Better control of image visualization.
- Standardization of two-dimensional physical comparison procedures.
- Improved reproducibility of results between separate examiners.
- Electronic transmission and archiving of image data.

MEASUREMENT OF PHYSICAL CHARACTERISTICS OF TWO- AND THREE-DIMENSIONAL EVIDENCE

The steps to create a digital comparison are described in this section. The examples are from forensic dentistry evaluations of bite mark evidence and dental identification of unidentified remains. The application of these methods may also be useful to other areas of forensic investigation that require image comparison information.

DIGITAL EVIDENCE 101

Image file storage

There are a number of storage systems through which forensic investigators can receive two-dimensional digital images of physical evidence. These include floppy disks, zipped (compressed) computer files, zip disks (100 MB or 250 MB storage capacity), compact disks (CD), email attachments and most often photographic prints, slides or negatives.

High-resolution scanning and digital camera settings

When a picture is in digital mode, as opposed to conventional film, the necessity to print the picture (hard copy) requires a "high resolution" setting for either the scanner or digital camera. The detail of a digital image is represented by the number of dots per inch (dpi) for scanners and digital cameras. Computer printers output these images in lines per inch (lpi). The computer storage necessary to store a photographic quality of $8\frac{1}{2}'' \times 11''$ picture is over 30 MB when 350 dpi is the selected resolution.

Archival images

Forensic digital imaging demands the examiner document each original image (i.e. case01original.jpg) and create a duplicate image for later use as a working copy (i.e. case01workingimage.jpg).

Image magnification using the computer monitor

Adobe Photoshop® is a retail software program that permits a multitude of editing features, functions, enhancements and metric (distances and angles) analysis. Once a crime scene photograph is scanned and imported into Photoshop, the initial working image can be enlarged using the zoom tool. Increments of 25% up to 300% and 400% enlargements may be shown on the computer monitor using this tool. The only limitation is the very high-resolution image (300 dpi) is required to avoid pixellation (fuzziness) of the magnified picture.

BITE MARKS

DIGITAL CONTROL OF PHOTOGRAPHIC DISTORTION EVIDENCE

The functional tools within Photoshop® can be used to detect and correct for certain angular distortions. This is an extremely important step as it forms the foundation for the comparison procedures that follow. The first issue with Figure 7.1 is the scale's off-angle position relative to the bite mark.

A photograph is a representation of the objects in the range of the camera lens. The degree to which this exactly reproduces those objects is influenced by many variables. When bite marks are photographed or dental radiographs are used as evidence, attempts are made to carefully control the off-angle camera placement in an effort to obtain an accurate picture of the bite mark or dental restoration for later forensic analysis. A tripod should be used whenever possible. Unfortunately, these efforts are not always successful and distortion is often introduced into the image from off-angle distortion.

Photography of bite marks and similar types of two- and three-dimensional physical evidence should have the following features:

- Presence of a scale (or some appropriate measuring device) oriented on the same plane as the bite mark or evidence sample.

Figure 7.1

The Adobe Photoshop®
working screen.

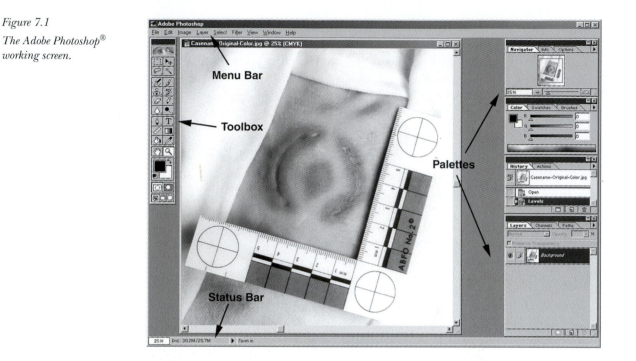

- The orientation of the camera (or film plane) and the scale is parallel.
- The scale is on the same plane as the bite mark thus eliminating parallax distortion. The scale is used to reproduce a life-size image of the object. Its displacement below or above the object will make this latter process inaccurate.

DETECTION OF PHOTOGRAPHIC DISTORTION BY THE FORENSIC EXAMINER

Correction for angular distortion focuses on the size and shape of the ruler present in the image. If the scale shows no distortion, then the evidence adjacent to it will be undistorted as well. The sides of the scale or ruler must be parallel, the incremental lines must be perpendicular to these sides and equally spaced and, if present, any circular reference shapes must be round (not an ellipse). A two-legged scale (a two-dimensional scale possessing an x-, y-axis) will have a 90° angle created at the intersection of the two legs. An ABFO No. 2 (Lightning Powder Co., Inc.) scale is shown in this chapter.

Placing a digital circle over the circular reference target and using it to evaluate the scale's sides, incremental lines and angles for parallelism can preliminarily check the degree of distortion (Figures 7.2 and 7.3).

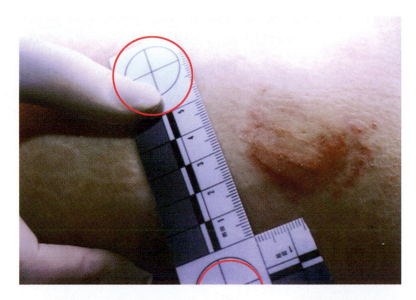

Figure 7.2

Evidence photograph showing a combination of photographic distortion. Type I distortion exists from the camera being mal-positioned over the injury. Type II results from the ABFO No. 2 scale not being completely parallel to either the camera and the bite mark. The red circles indicate the elliptical shape of the scale's top circular reference point and the circular shape of the lower reference point.

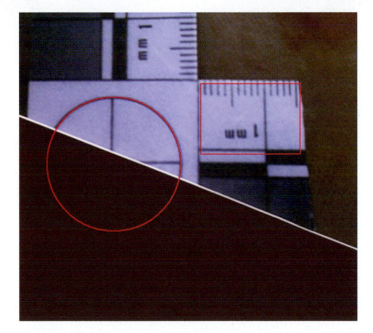

Figure 7.3

In this case, the corner of the ABFO No. 2 scale is in the same plane as the injury pattern. The 1.5 cm portion of the scale's lower edge can be used to establish the life-size dimensions of the picture.

Simple rotation and cropping of the bite mark image

The evidence image must have the scale oriented along the x- and y-axis of the entire image in order to perform later manipulation based on this scale. Excess perimeters in the image may be removed using the crop tool (Figure 7.4).

Figure 7.4

The evidence image in Figure 7.2 corrected to proper 1 : 1 (life-size) dimensions. The useable portion of the scale (the lower corner) is dimensionally corrected to 1.5 cm using Photoshop®. This is dependent on the injury pattern being in the same plane as that portion of the scale.

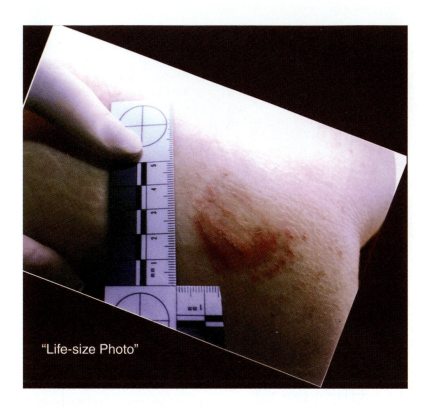

Determination of Theta

Before attempts can be made to digitally correct the off-angle camera positioning, the amount of distortion should be measured. The examiner evaluating the bite mark photograph should refer to the circular reference shapes present on the scale. An elliptical shape proves the camera-positioning angle was incorrect. The amount of non-parallelism (theta) is determined by:

1. Measuring a line across the narrowest distance of the ellipse (minor axis A).
2. Measuring a line across the major axis of the ellipse (major axis B).

The angle theta may be determined by solving theta $= \cos^{-1} A/B$ (Figures 7.5 and 7.6).

Correcting the photographic distortion

If it has been determined that significant distortion exists, it must be corrected before the bite mark photograph is resized and/or enhanced. Only then can a meaningful comparison analysis be accomplished. Correction may be accomplished by an experienced photographic technician or digital imaging technician.

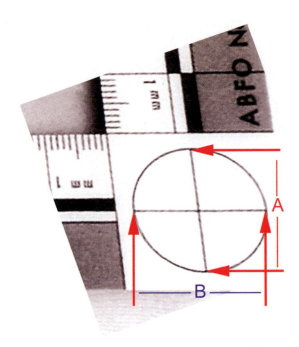

Figure 7.5

Off-angle camera placement has made the normally circular reference an ellipse. Measurements of the A (minor axis) and B (major axis) create a ratio that can be used to determine Theta.

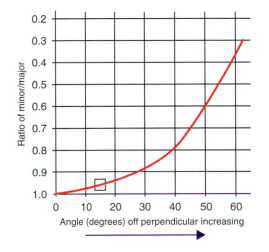

Figure 7.6

Determining Theta. The ratio of the distance A (minor axis) to B (major axis) is 0.94. Find this value of the vertical scale of this graph and draw a horizontal line right until it meets the red curved line. The Theta value (amount of off-angle camera placement) in this example is about 15° (black box on the red line).

Definitions of photographic distortion

Type I distortion

The scale and bite mark are on plane but the camera back is not parallel to either (Figure 7.7).

This non-parallelism of the camera can be corrected. When the image of the scale is brought back to its original size and shape, the image of the bite mark will also be corrected (rectification). This assumes that the scale itself is on a single plane and there is no parallax distortion relative to the bite mark.

Figure 7.7
Type I distortion.

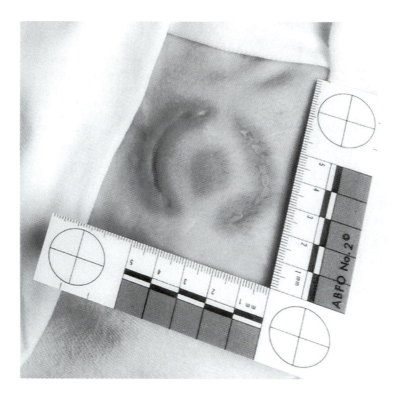

Type II distortion

If the scale is not on the same plane as the bite mark, rectifying the scale will adversely affect the proportions of the injury pattern. In situations like this, it is best not to try to rectify the scale but perform the resize (1:1) procedure based on the scale "as is".

The amount of parallax distortion present will obviously affect the accuracy of the results. The weight given to the results will contribute to the ultimate decision in the case. The investigator must decide what amount of distortion is acceptable in order to produce a meaningful comparison. Figure 7.2 is an example of this type of distortion that is still amenable to correction.

Type III distortion

In some cases, one leg of a two-dimensional scale will have perspective distortion but the other leg will not (Figure 7.8).

Type IV distortion

In this instance, the scale itself may be bent or skewed. There can be forensic value if the scale is relatively flat in the area directly adjacent to the bite mark.

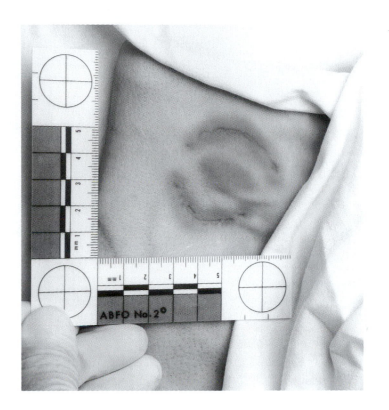

Figure 7.8
Type III distortion.

Peripheral scale inaccuracies can be discounted. Use only the area next to the mark for the resizing procedures. Do not use the entire scale. There must be at least a 1 cm length of non-distorted scale in close proximity to the bite mark (Figure 7.9).

Limitations

Cases occur when an image is so severely distorted, due to poor photographic technique, there is no forensic value. The subject matter must be re-photographed but unfortunately, sometimes the physical evidence has changed or disappeared, thus preventing these remedial efforts.

It is important to realize which type of distortion, if any, is present within the original bite mark photograph. This can often be a difficult task and requires some experience. Another concern is the utilization of a two-dimensional object (the scale) to analyze a three-dimensional bite mark. It is a very significant concern with a bite mark on a curved surface.

The variations present in bite mark cases present challenges to the examiner regarding the value of the injury pattern and the relationship to a suspect(s) teeth. Photoshop® can help in a large number of these cases but, again, it is the

Figure 7.9

Type IV distortion. The bent areas of the scale are not used in resizing the image.

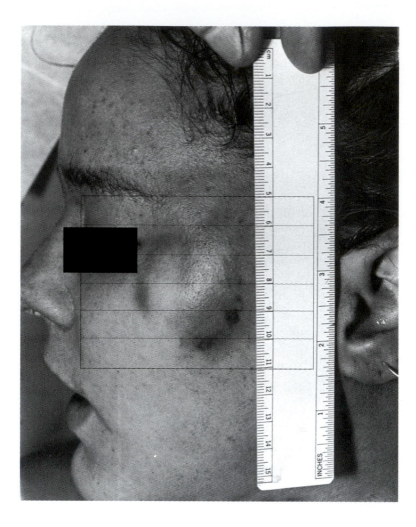

investigator who must determine the limits to the use of bite mark evidence and its impact on the strength of the ultimate opinion.

COMPUTER GENERATED EXEMPLARS OF A SUSPECT DENTITION

Simple overlay

A major purpose of using digital imaging is to produce a properly rectified (no off-angle distortion), scaled, reproduction of a suspect's tooth biting edges. The term Hollow Volume refers to the outline or perimeter of each biting surface. This product is called an overlay. The final process is to place the overlay onto the bite mark evidence and evaluate the physical correspondence between the two. The increased accuracy of this digital process is the chief

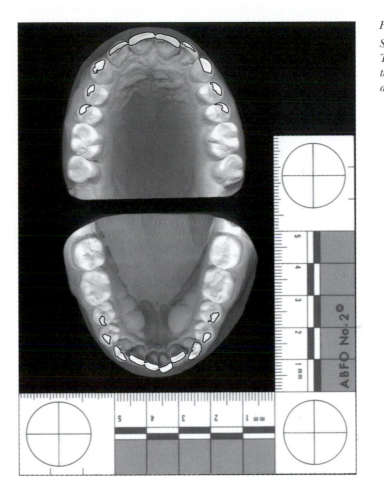

Figure 7.10
Scan of dental models.
The outline of the front
teeth has been selected
as a black outline.

improvement over the conventional methods of overlay production. The dental examiner uses the computer program to select the dental biting edges instead of using hand drawn tracings of the suspect plaster models (Figure 7.10). From this selection of the biting edges of the teeth, their outline is used to produce the computer-generated overlay (Figure 7.11).

DIGITAL COMPARISON OF BITE MARK EVIDENCE

Completion of the analysis occurs when the digital overlay is superimposed onto the bite mark image. In this example, the correlation between the two is extremely high. This is because the bite mark was made experimentally and the actual biter's teeth were used for this comparison (Figures 7.12 and 7.13).

Figure 7.11

The selected teeth outlines and case information can be created as its own document for later superimposition (after being reversed) onto the bite mark.

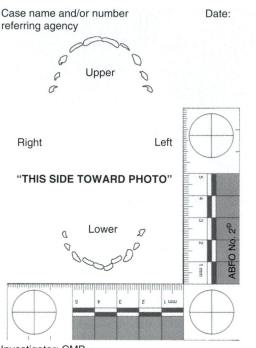

Case name and/or number referring agency

Date:

Upper

Right   Left

"THIS SIDE TOWARD PHOTO"

Lower

Investigator: CMB

Figure 7.12

The overlay has been reversed and then placed onto the bite mark image. The identification value of this comparison is extremely high. The bite mark was experimentally created and the teeth used in this comparison are of the actual biter.

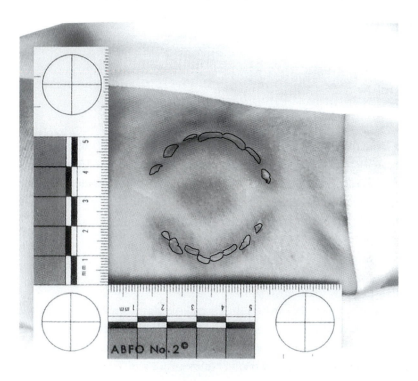

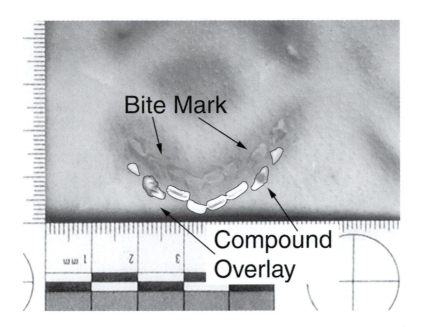

Figure 7.13
The "compound overlay" is more than the outline of teeth. It incorporates all of the two-dimensional image values of the dental models.

METRIC ANALYSIS OF BITE MARK INJURIES

The use of digital imaging allows the examiner to measure physical data in bite mark cases. The application of certain Photoshop tools and functions provide the dental examiner with physical evidence data that will create linear and angular information useful to support the final conclusions regarding a case.

Bite mark injuries *and* suspect(s) teeth possess pertinent physical characteristics, which are amenable to digital measurement. The most obvious are:

- Arch width (distance from one cuspid across to the other cuspid).
- Shape of the dental arch (generally can be described as C-shaped, oval, or U-shaped).
- Labiolingual position (a tooth out of normal alignment anterior posteriorly).
- Rotational position (twisted).
- Intertooth spacing.
- Tooth width and thickness.
- Curvatures of biting edges.
- Wear patterns and unusual dental anatomy.

Step 1: Analysis of a bite mark injury

It is recommended that the injury pattern be completely analyzed before the dentition of a suspect(s) is evaluated. This insures a measure of blindness when features of the injury are vague and ambiguous. This establishes hard data sets

Figure 7.14

An actual case involving a bite mark analysis. The numbers indicate upper teeth that are identifiable in the bite mark. The lines are drawn to measure distances and angles created by these teeth for correlation with possible biters.

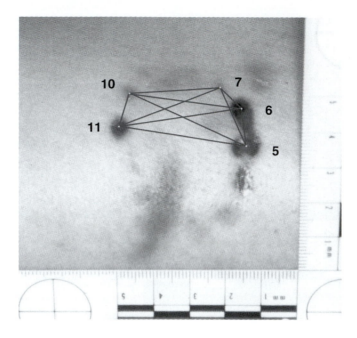

for this questioned sample before commencing the analysis of the suspect's teeth (Figure 7.14).

- Cuspid to cuspid.
- x/y-axis.
- Tooth-widths and thickness.
- Rotational value of each tooth.

Step 2: Analyzing the suspect dentition

Identical steps are then performed using the scanned images of the suspect's plaster dental casts (Figure 7.15). Metric analysis of dentition casts using the following features of each tooth.

- Cuspid to cuspid distance.
- x/y-axis and inter tooth distances.
- Tooth-widths and thicknesses.
- Rotational value of each tooth.

Step 3: Comparison data of a hypothetical case

Bite mark: Upper jaw width   Suspect: Upper jaw width

42 mm   42 mm

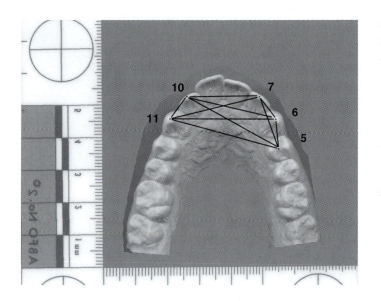

Figure 7.15

Suspect dental analysis. Due to the limitations of information available in the bite mark, the suspect's upper teeth are analyzed in the same manner. There is correlation between the two evidence samples, but there is not enough data available to make a positive bite mark identification.

The examiner should create a total profile of features for both evidence types (suspect and known) to support the final conclusion in the case.

DENTAL IDENTIFICATION: THE USES OF DIGITAL IMAGING

The methods described above may also be applied for the superimposition of dental and medical X-rays that are pertinent to human identification cases. The following case studies indicate the usefulness of digital superimposition[1].

CASE ONE

The unidentified human remains consisted of a complete maxilla and mandible with all adult teeth present. The only restoration present was a distal pit amalgam on tooth #3 (Figure 7.16). The known dental records obtained for comparison belonged to a female sub-adult dated 7 years earlier (Figure 7.17). The antemortem radiographs (4 bitewings) showed predominantly primary teeth present with the exception of all four permanent first molars. A distal pit metallic restoration (silver amalgam) was present on tooth #3. All other teeth present within the radiographs were not restored and showed no unusual shapes. The identification focused on tooth #3 due to the fact that the primary (baby) teeth had fallen out, the scarcity of restorations present and the paucity of antemortem records (Figures 7.18 and 7.19).

Figure 7.16

Postmortem radiograph of an unknown deceased showing a metal dental restoration in tooth #3.

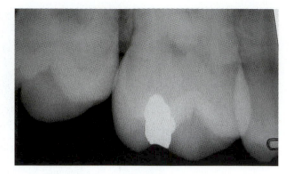

Figure 7.17

Antemortem radiograph of a known person showing a metal dental restoration in tooth #3.

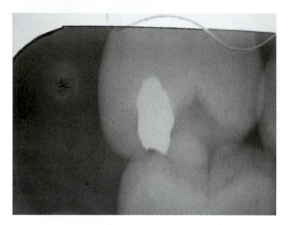

Figure 7.18

The postmortem filling (black) is superimposed onto the white antemortem filling in the back ground.

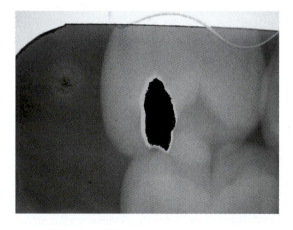

The antemortem radiograph was severely elongated due to improper angulation of the X-ray beam. The postmortem radiograph showed a more normal orientation. Despite these differences, the restorations did show similarities in relative shape.

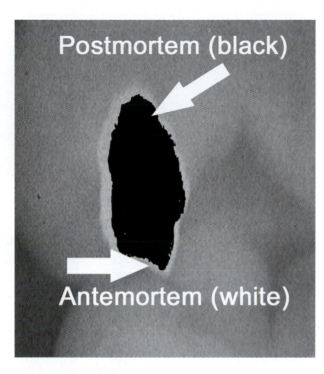

Figure 7.19

The perimeter detail of the two fillings is significantly similar.

Results

Based on the comparison of the restoration on tooth #3 and the physical characteristics of the human remains (sex, age, height, etc.), it was concluded that the antemortem and postmortem dental evidence originated from the same individual.

CASE TWO

The recovered unknown human remains were fragmented due to trauma from a high-energy impact. The lower right human jaw fragment contained only two molar teeth (FDI #46 and 47; Universal numbering system: #30 and #31). Tooth #30 had separate occlusal and buccal restorations (silver amalgam). Tooth #31 had an occlusal amalgam restoration. A check of missing persons lists that fit the known physical and circumstantial details of the recovered deceased provided one set of antemortem records as a possible identity. These known antemortem records consisted of a written treatment record and four bitewing radiographs. These records predated the discovery of the human remains by 10 years. The antemortem radiographs showed tooth #30 with a buccal (or lingual) metallic restoration (most likely amalgam). These dental restorations provided no help with the identification process due to: (1) the age of the

Figure 7.20

Each image was separately rotated to create an identical horizontal orientation for the antemortem and postmortem evidence (also see Figure 7.21).

Figure 7.21

Post-rotation images with the CEJ of tooth #31 defining the x-axis.

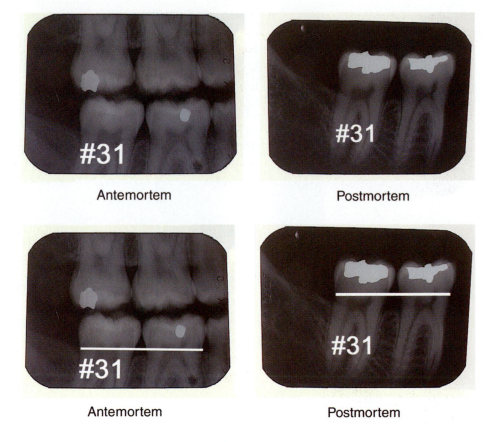

Antemortem   Postmortem

Antemortem   Postmortem

antemortem records and (2) additional restored surfaces seen in the postmortem remains.

The dental remains were radiographed at three different angles. This produced one X-ray that was close to the tooth angulation seen in the antemortem radiograph selected for analysis. These images were scanned and imported into Adobe Photoshop®. Figure 7.20 shows an antemortem and a postmortem image that were selected for comparison based on their physical similarity.

Once digitized, both images were opened in the imaging program, adjusted to equivalent resolutions (300 dpi) and placed side-by-side (tiled) on the computer monitor. Present in both images was the cemento-enamel junction (CEJ) of tooth #31. This feature was chosen as the mutual horizontal plane of orientation. Figure 21 shows a line connecting the respective mesial and distal CEJ of #31 before digital rotation to the same x-axis. This x–y orientation was necessary to use the image program's digital resizing capabilities.

The antemortem CEJ dimension "A" was selected as the resize control and calculated in centimeters. The postmortem CEJ dimension "a" was similarly measured (Figures 7.22 and 7.23). The ratio A/a was used to resize the postmortem image to match the antemortem CEJ dimension. Metric analysis was

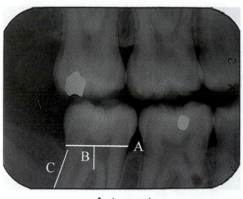

Antemortem

Figure 7.22

Antemortem image showing the CEJ dimension "A", root furcation height "B" and distal root divergence angle "C".

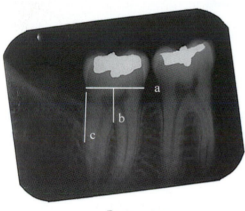

Postmortem

Figure 7.23

Postmortem image showing CEJ dimension "a", root furcation height "b" and distal root divergence angle "c".

carried out for two non-age-dependent parameters for each image's root system: (1) root furcation heights, measured from the height of the furcation to the level of the CEJ ("B", "b") and (2) distal root divergence angles ("C", "c").

These parameters were measured for teeth #30 and #31 in both the antemortem and postmortem radiographs. The results were compared in Table 7.1.

The postmortem image was moved onto the antemortem image for a shape comparison evaluation (Figure 7.24). The images were superimposed using the CEJ planes as the common reference. Changing the opacity of the postmortem (top) layer allows visualization of the similarities and differences between the two images.

Table 7.1

Antemortem	
A (cm)	2.24
B (cm)	0.82
C (degrees)	70.3
Postmortem	
a (cm)	2.24
b (cm)	1.32
c (degrees)	88.0

Results

There were several physical similarities between the antemortem and postmortem dental features seen on the radiographs. Digital analysis, however,

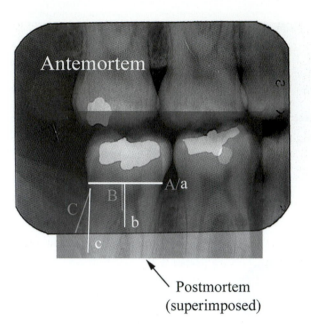

revealed significant differences of tooth shapes. The root divergence angle differed by 12.8°. The root height differed by 32%. It was concluded, based on these factors alone, that the antemortem dental records and postmortem dental evidence did *not* come from the same individual.

CASE THREE

The decomposed body of an elderly male was found floating in the ocean outside a harbor. No personal identification was in the clothing and the body was transported to the Ventura County medical examiner's office for examination.

Autopsy disclosed advanced decomposition with bloating and multiple areas of postmortem marine animal depredation. Postmortem loss of tissue from the right wrist revealed a stainless steel orthopedic fixation device on his radius. The dentition was severely carious with many teeth missing and no evidence of dental restorations. Fair quality fingerprints were obtained but no matching prints were found in fingerprint databases. None of the local law enforcement agencies had records of missing persons matching the general characteristics of the decedent during the prior month.

The medical examiner released the general information about the decedent to the local press, along with a description of his clothing and the orthopedic device. An adult daughter of the decedent called the medical examiner after reading the news release and provided a description of her father who had been missing for three weeks. The physical description was consistent and the daughter recognized some of the clothing. She also recalled that her father had

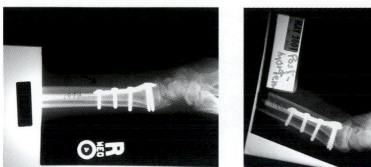

Antemortem   Postmortem

Figure 7.25

Images consisted of the antemortem forearm radiograph (labeled 1994) and the postmortem forearm radiograph (labeled 2001).

broken his wrist several years prior. Calls to several hospitals led to finding a radiograph of the decedent's right wrist that was taken after placement of an orthopedic device for stabilizing a fracture seven years prior to his death. Postmortem radiographs of the forearm produced images of the orthopedic device that were very similar to the antemortem films. This was believed sufficient to establish the identification. The original image objects analyzed are shown in Figure 7.25.

Checking the reference shapes for angular photographic distortion

Radio-opaque labels were contained within each of the two radiographs for the purpose of orientation, identification, and size verification. Each of these reference labels consists of the letter "R" above a three-letter sequence. A circular reference shape lies below the identification letters. This circle has an outside dimension of 1.5 cm. Angular distortion occurs when the object being photographed or radiographed is not perpendicular to the film or X-ray beam. This distortion is revealed when the object within the resultant image is not its real life-size and/or shape.

The reference objects in both the antemortem and postmortem images are circular thereby indicating no photographic distortion in these images. This was confirmed by superimposing a digitally created perfect circle over the reference shape. This procedure was carried out for both the antemortem (1994) and postmortem (2001) images. Figure 7.26 illustrates this technique. The image size for the antemortem and postmortem radiographs was then corrected to life-size (1 : 1).

Digital superimposition of the antemortem and postmortem devices

The postmortem device was then digitally colored black (Figure 7.27) and placed on top of the antemortem device (Figure 7.28).

Figure 7.26

The black circle was digitally created to assess the symmetry of the X-ray reference object.

Figure 7.27

The postmortem device is colored black to contrast with the antemortem X-ray.

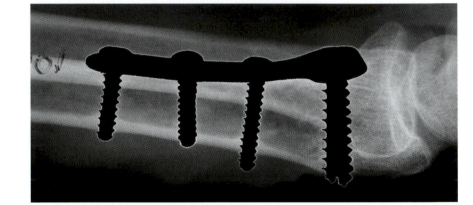

Figure 7.28

This initial superimposition revealed noticeable linear and angular differences between the antemortem and postmortem device images. This was caused by differing positions of the forearm on the film cassette between the two radiographic sessions (1994 and 2001). This is called Type II distortion.

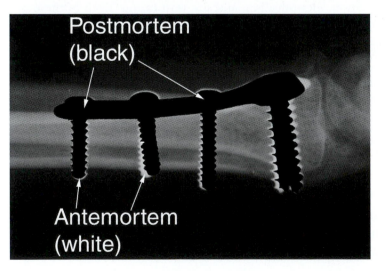

Digital analysis affords an option, which is to assume that the antemortem image of the device is correct and use those dimensions to resize the unknown (postmortem) image. A comparison of the two images based on this reference would then allow the investigator to analyze other similarities and discrepancies

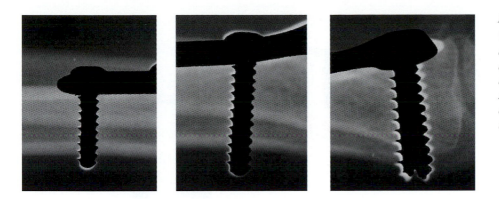

Figure 7.29

Three sections of the comparison are viewed after digital adjustments are made to correct for slight dimension differences between the two X-rays.

between the two samples. Specifically, the outline contours, relative dimensions, angular relationship of the device components and individual contours of the components can then be compared. This method was chosen for this case.

The relative position of device components (angular and dimensional relationships of screws, etc.) and specific outline characteristics can now be compared.

Visual comparison

The general size and shape of the postmortem device shows a high degree of concordance with the antemortem device. There was good agreement when more specific features (individual screw threads) were compared.

Photoshop® can correct for the majority of photographic distortion but there can still be minor angular differences remaining after the rectification process. This is especially true when comparing images with large amounts of angular discrepancies and/or three-dimensional curved surfaces. This case falls into both these categories. In order to accurately compare the screw thread outlines, slight alignment adjustments must be made when different areas are analyzed. It is unrealistic to expect the entire image to exactly superimpose in this type of analysis due to subtle differences in the radiographic samples. Sectional analysis is advised in this circumstance (Figure 7.29).

Determination of identity

One of the major advantages of digital image analysis is the ability to quantify concordant and/or dissimilar features. Although visual comparisons as described above can be extremely helpful, the addition of quantitative analyses can provide a more objective result.

The task is to first find the area (in pixels) of the antemortem device image. The same is done for the rectified postmortem image. Following superimposition, the degree of commonality can be quantified by the percentage of pixels the two samples share. Figure 7.30 shows colorized images of the two devices.

Figure 7.30

The number of pixels within each color image are counted and then compared for concordant values. The use of digital comparison methods helps the investigator control dimension variables during the comparison of physical objects. In this case, the identification was confirmed by other means, with this portion of the investigation being supportive of the final decision.

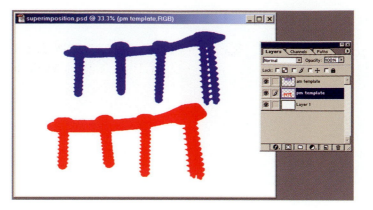

	# of pixels	Common pixels (%)
Antemortem template (blue)	177,975	92
Postmortem template (red)	197,559	83
Common pixels (purple)	164,136	

Figure 7.31

The postmortem device template (blue) is superimposed on the antemortem (red) device template and aligned. The opacity of the postmortem template layer is reduced to allow visualization of the antemortem layer below. The common pixels will appear purple in color.

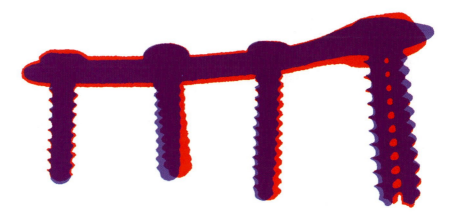

The table in Figure 7.30 shows the results of the comparison of the antemortem and postmortem orthopedic devices. The degree of common pixels (placing the blue image over the red image produces the color purple) indicates the commonality of the two devices (Figure 7.31). The differences between the two, which visually appears quite similar, are now quantified.

REFERENCE

1. Bowers CM, Johansen RJ. Digital imaging methods as an aid in dental identification of human remains. *J Forensic Sci*. 2002; 47(2): 354–359. Reprint permission granted by ASTM, Inc.

CHAPTER 8

LEGAL ISSUES IN FORENSIC ODONTOLOGY

Law enforcement and other disciplines should understand, in a non-lawyer way, how experts and courts view the introduction and describe their findings regarding forensic odontology. This chapter gives an overview on these subjects. Dental identification has a legal history with little disagreement. The history of identification from bite marks requires considerable caution in its use in the legal arena and is a major subject of this chapter. Later in this chapter, there is a review of the odontological literature that is used to support what dentists say about bite mark identification.

LEGAL FACTORS OF EVIDENCE COLLECTION AND ITS USE IN COURT

The focus of this book is on collection techniques and methods for forensic investigation involving dental evidence. Just as important are the legal steps necessary to make sure efforts in the field and laboratory are allowed into court proceedings.

The typical criminal proceeding in the US has the prosecution introducing evidence that either directly or indirectly (by assumption) implicates someone as the actor of a crime. It is obvious that the best defense for such accusations of guilt is to get the court to refuse to accept it at trial. The argument of inadmissibility is the defense counsel's strongest argument before the trial even begins. The defense also has the privilege to introduce forensic evidence supporting their arguments.

The legal basis for a motion to deny evidence (e.g. to exclude) at trial is that the proponent (the person wanting it admitted) violated the defendant's constitutional right to protection against an unlawful search or seizure by the police. Evidence resulting from this illegal search or seizure is also subject to exclusion. The general rules regarding this are important for the investigator to understand.

Forensic Dental Evidence
ISBN: 0-1212-1042-1

THE FOURTH AMENDMENT: ARREST SEARCH AND SEIZURE

The Fourth Amendment applies to both state and federal law enforcement. It reads, "The right of the people to be secure in their persons, houses, papers, and effects, against unreasonable searches and seizures shall not be violated, and no warrants shall issue, but upon probable cause, supported by oath or affirmation, and specifically describing the place to be searched, and the person or things to be seized".

THE EXCLUSIONARY RULE

This is the rule that is argued in court when law enforcement fail to follow proper procedure in collecting evidence. The rule states, "Evidence that is obtained by unreasonable search or seizure must be excluded from evidence". Evidence obtained by private parties is not subject to the Exclusionary Rule.

FRUITS OF THE POISONOUS TREE

This colorful phrase prevents the state from using *any* evidence remotely derived from other illegally obtained evidence.

SEARCH WARRANT DETAILS

The specificity requirement of this rule provides that items to be seized must be described with as much particularity as reasonably possible. Obtaining dental evidence from a person falls under this rule.

Protecting the evidence involves numerous procedural steps that agencies should already have in place prior to performing any search. Dental evidence at a scene is lawfully obtained via these steps. Please consult these procedures prior to conducting any evidence collection.

Evidence taken from a suspect must also pass muster in the legal arena. The most common means of doing this is to get the subject's written permission (e.g. an informed consent) to obtain evidence or to have a court order approved for the specific types of evidence (saliva swab, dental impressions, etc.) needed. The methods used to obtain this evidence should also be clearly written and described in the consent or court order. Early bite mark cases had subjects refusing to admit to dental impressions. This has not been considered a valid objection in the US, in that the procedure is not invasive (e.g. surgical or dangerous), the dental information is reasonable and not considered a means of self-incrimination (e.g. the subject being forced to testify against his interests) violating the Fifth Amendment to the US Constitution.

TYPES OF DENTAL TESTIMONY BY DENTISTS

Dentists testify in criminal cases about dental identification of the deceased or the identification of biters from tooth marks.

WHO CAN TESTIFY AS AN EXPERT ON BITE MARK EVIDENCE

The courts consider an expert to be a person whose knowledge, training and experience creates an understanding of facts that are outside the abilities of the average individual. This knowledge must be relevant (be related) to the question being asked in court, such as, "Is this injury a human bite mark?" or "Did this particular automobile tire fail and cause the accident?". This knowledge has to help the judge and the jury in rendering a verdict. Using this simple test, people possessing many skills are allowed into the courtroom, such as dentists, automobile tire engineers, policemen and plumbers. The expert, once admitted, is allowed to render an opinion on matters that occurred outside his/her presence. This is a very powerful and important tool in criminal cases where quite often both the prosecution and defense counsel have their own experts whose opinions do not agree. Experts actually reconstruct, to the best of their ability, the events that occurred during an act related to a crime. Certainly, regarding dental evidence, the best information for a court is from a certified forensic odontologist.

WHAT MAKES A DENTIST A FORENSIC EXPERT?

Forensic dentistry is not recognized by the American Dental Association as a dental specialty. This attitude varies between countries. The UK has established a court certification for all forensic experts. Law enforcement, however, has relied on dentists who assist them to be competent and familiar with forensic protocols.

The typical forensic dental expert is a practicing dentist or a dental educator. A handful of dentists work for federal agencies. The US military has active duty dentists forensically trained through the Armed Forces Institute of Pathology (AFIP) at most major bases.

The professional forensic organizations where most practicing forensic dentists belong are the American Academy of Forensic Sciences (AAFS) and the American Society of Forensic Odontology (ASFO). The AAFS has an odontology section with a membership of over 300 dentists. Their experience varies from Trainee to Fellow. The ASFO has a membership of over 1,000. This includes dentists, dental hygienists and anyone interested in forensic odontology.

SHORT HISTORY OF BITEMARK EVIDENCE IN THE US' COURTS

Bitemark analysis is a product of the latter half of the 20th century. The small number of dentists in early court bite mark proceedings has increased substantially over the last 25 years. The physical evidence available in a bite mark case is challenging and requires the dentists to exercise extreme care in their opinions. The vast array of potential biters can be large due to the fragmentary and diffuse bruising regularly seen in skin injuries. Bite marks in food, however, have a better potential for tooth detail.

COURT ADMISSIBILITY OF BITE MARK OPINIONS

This information deals with the legal acceptance of bite mark analysis in the State of California. Others states and countries have differing histories and legal thinking regarding scientific evidence. In California in 1975, *Marx* was higher court review of a case where bite mark identification was allowed into court. The higher court's opinion considered it a "new" science and subject to review.

California law requires that before evidence of a "new" scientific technique can be admissible, the giver of the evidence must show that the relevant scientific community deems the technique reliable. The California Supreme Court in the case of *People v. Kelly* established this rule of law (1976). In the *Kelly* case, the California Supreme Court further refined the rule previously made by the US Supreme Court in the 1923 case, *Frye v. US.*

The *Frye* case involved evidence of a systolic blood pressure deception test which was found by the US Supreme Court to be inadmissible because the test had not gained general acceptance in the particular field in which it belongs. The California Supreme Court, in *Kelly*, rejected voiceprint evidence because the evidence in favor failed to establish that the procedure was accepted as reliable by the relevant scientific community. The California Court stated that to meet the standard of admissibility, the offering party must establish:

1. The generally accepted reliability of the methods;
2. That the witnesses furnishing testimony are properly qualified by an expert to give an opinion; and
3. It must be demonstrated that the correct scientific procedures were used.

The California Supreme Court also stated in the *People v. Kelly* opinion that:

> Once a trial court has admitted evidence based on a new scientific technique, and that decision is affirmed on appeal by a published appellate decision,

the precedent so established may control subsequent trials, at least until new
evidence is presented reflecting a change in the attitude of the scientific
community. *People v. Kelly* (1976).

California appellate courts had no problem finding that bite mark evidence
is an admissible and reliable evidence. One of the first cases to address the issue
was *People v. Marx* (1975). In this post-*Frye*, pre-*Kelly* case, the Second District
Court of Appeal noted "The Frye test finds its rational basis in the degree to
which the trier of fact must accept on faith, scientific hypothesis not capable
of proof or disproof in court and not even generally accepted outside the
courtroom".

In *Marx*, the court's findings were that in the case of the bite mark evidence,
the basic data on which the experts based their conclusions were acceptable to
the court – which included models, photos and X-rays of the victim's wounds
and the defendant's teeth – and that in making their comparisons and reaching
their conclusions, the experts did not rely on untested methods or unproven
hypotheses, but applied scientifically and professionally established techniques
so that the court did not have to sacrifice its independence and common
sense in evaluating it.

In 1977, the First District Court of Appeals upheld the admissibility of bite
mark evidence in the case of *People v. Watson* (1977). In *Watson*, the court relied
heavily on the Marx case, which was cited as the setting proper precedent.

The next significant case addressing the admissibility of bite mark evidence was
People v. Slone (1978). In this Second District case, the court found that the bite
mark identification evidence admitted by the trial court met the three-pronged
test of admissibility laid down by *Kelly*. The court cited the Marx case and reiter-
ated its analysis that there is a more trustworthy basis for admitting bite mark
evidence than other scientific test evidence. The superior trustworthiness is due to
the trier of fact seeing for itself by looking at the material exhibits what constitutes
the basis for comparison with a defendant's dentition.

USE OF BITE MARK EVIDENCE IN JURISDICTIONS USING THE FRYE STANDARD FOR ADMISSIBILITY

Appellate courts throughout the US have routinely determined that bite mark
evidence is reliable and has been accepted as such by the relevant scientific
community. Following is a sampling of cases from various jurisdictions, which
have all approved the admissibility of bite mark evidence.

1. *Doyle v. State* (1954): In this case, the Texas Court of Criminal Appeals upheld
   the admissibility of bite mark evidence. In that case, before trial the dentist

examined bite marks in two pieces of cheese left at the scene of burglary of a market and compared them as seen in a plaster model of a bite mark made by the defendant in a piece of cheese provided him by the Sheriff. The dentist determined that the same teeth made all the bite marks. Similar identification methods had been used for years.

2. *Niehaus v. State of Indiana* (1977): The Supreme Court of Indiana found no error in the trial court's admission of bite mark evidence. In *Niehaus*, a forensic odontologist compared a bite mark in the victim's skin to the teeth of the defendant. The court noted that the method of identification "is simply a comparison of items of physical evidence to determine if they are reciprocal. The methods consist of standardized procedures known to procure accurate models and measurements".

3. *State v. Sager* (1980): The Missouri Court of Appeals presents a thorough treatment of the evolution of bite mark in its decision in *State v. Sager*. The *Sager* case involved the murder of a 14-year-old girl. The State's evidence included comparisons by forensic odontologists, of bite marks on the victim's body to the defendant's dentition. After a painstaking review of voluminous legal and dental authorities, the Missouri Court determined that "the science of positive bite mark identification has reached the level of scientific reliability and credibility to permit its admission as evidence in criminal proceedings".

All of these and hundreds of similar cases from the 1970s and 1980s show the courts' interest and approval in bite mark identifications. It may be surprising to some, though, that the scientific research necessary to ground such opinion as reliable had yet to be undertaken. The "acceptance by the scientific community" thrust of *Frye*, however, was clearly met by the majority of the forensic dental community of the time.

Little has changed in bite mark analysis appellate opinions since. Legal commentaries have been critical of bite mark identification since the 1970s but to date have had little effect in eliminating bite mark opinions. The legal analysis of the *Marx* decision from a more scientifically critical position holds that the court's statement was "no established science of identifying persons from bite marks" was overlooked in their final conclusion ruling bite mark evidence admissible. This conflicts with the underlying reason that experts are allowed into court since they know more than the average person on a certain subject. The tools used in the Marx case were considered appropriate and then the court allowed the reasoning or application of these tools to be admitted, the reliability requirements of *Kelly* notwithstanding. This argument still exists in the 21st century as it is generally brought to court during every trial containing bite mark evidence. The advent of DNA analysis has recently acted as an independent means to support or refute a bite mark opinion. In some cases, it has helped the proponents of bite mark identification and in other cases, it proves that bite mark identification is subjective and cannot be counted on as being accurate in every case.

USE OF BITE MARK TESTIMONY UNDER THE FEDERAL RULES OF EVIDENCE

The Federal judicial system has numerous rules and opinion on the accuracy and credibility of experts and the opinions that they provide in court.* The Federal system within the last 10 years has rejected the *Frye* standard and created a new standard based on the case named *Daubert*. The *Daubert* ruling rests on an interpretation of the Federal Rules of Evidence. These rules are not binding on the state court system, but a number of states have adopted a similar standard (Table 8.1).

Daubert considers four factors: (1) testability of the methods used, (2) error rate determination of these methods and results. Errors in odontology can either be a misidentification from teeth or a bite mark (false positive id) or the rejection of the true identity or biter (false negative id), (3) the acceptance of the methods by the appropriate scientific community, and (4) presence of relevant peer review and publication on the subject. Appropriate questions can also include:

1. What are the expert's qualifications and stature in the scientific community?
2. Can other experts repeat the same methods and reach the same results?
3. Can the technique and its results be explained with sufficient clarity so the judge and jury can understand its plain meaning?

All these factors are considered independent determinations by the court and do not have to be met by the expert. What is not satisfied, however, may affect the weight or value of the expert's testimony. It should be noted that, as of this

* Federal Rules of Evidence 702: Testimony by experts, "If scientific, technical, or other specialized knowledge will assist the trier of fact to understand the evidence or to determine a fact in issue, a witness qualified as an expert by knowledge, skill, experience training, or education may testify hereto in the form of an opinion or otherwise".

States using Daubert	States still using Frye	Other
Connecticut	Alaska	Arkansas
Indiana	Arizona	Delaware
Kentucky	California	Georgia
Louisiana	Colorado	Iowa
Massachusetts	Florida	Minnesota
New Mexico	Illinois	Montana
Oklahoma	Kansas	North Carolina
South Dakota	Maryland	Oregon
Texas	Michigan	Utah
West Virginia	Missouri	Vermont
	Nebraska	Wyoming
	New York	
	Pennsylvania	
	Washington	

Table 8.1

States using Daubert, Frye, *or other admissibility tests.*

writing (2003), no Federal court has reviewed bite mark evidence under these requirements. A few states have done so, with no change in the *cart blanche* admissibility permitted since 1954.

TYPICAL QUESTIONS LAW ENFORCEMENT ASKS REGARDING DENTAL EVIDENCE

CAN A NON-BOARD CERTIFIED DENTIST BE CONSIDERED A FORENSIC EXPERT?

The simplest rule to remember is that anyone who can help the court and jury make a decision and has appropriate credentials can be admitted as an expert. What will vary is the importance (weight) the jury gives to the testimony given by a non-certified or novice forensic expert.

HOW MUCH TRAINING DOES A DENTIST NEED BEFORE TESTIFYING IN COURT?

Law enforcement should know that the traditional dental education fails to provide the dentist with skills necessary to perform in the judicial system and many aspects of forensic science. Simple dental identification cases of unknown deceased persons require competency skills any licensed dentist should possess. Bite mark evidence, mass disaster management and determination of child, elder, or spousal abuse should be handled by an experienced forensic odontologist.

CAN JUST ONE PERSON BE IDENTIFIED FROM BITING SOMETHING?

The best means of identifying a biter is to swab the bitten object for saliva and then obtained a DNA profile from the biologist. The history of bite mark analysis shows a number of cases over the years where an expert's confident positive bite mark identification of a defendant has been proven wrong. Most experienced odontologists say that the ability to positively identify one person from a bite mark is a very rare event. The typical bite mark case contains the argument that a particular person "possibly" or "probably" created a bite mark.

THE SCIENTIFIC LIMITATIONS OF BITE MARK TESTIMONY

The determination of a positive identification by bite mark analysis is limited by the quality of the physical evidence, the variable nature of bruising in skin, and the inability of dentists to scientifically prove that everyone's teeth are unique. The following outlines these issues in more detail.

ACCURACY OF SKIN FOR BITE MARKS

In cases of physical assaults having skin injuries, the variables that make each bite mark case challenging includes:

1. The anatomy bitten.
2. The biology of skin injuries.
3. Posture of victim during biting.
4. Poor bruising detail of the bite injury on skin.

DENTAL PROFILING THAT CANNOT PROVE UNIQUENESS

The foundation of bite mark analysis is that the total arrangement of a person's teeth (usually the front teeth) creates a dental profile. There are arguments in the dental literature that each human has a unique dental profile that is discernible in bite marks. This has not been proven valid either by experimental testing or by bite mark casework. Cases having DNA evidence that contradict a bite mark opinion are becoming more common and should act as a indicator that bite mark identification cannot solely give a conclusive answer to the question, "Who made this bite mark?". At best, the most conservative approach taken is that it can include or exclude a person.

BITE MARK GUIDELINES

The ABFO Bite Mark Guidelines and Standards express technique recommendations and establish limits on the language and procedures used by forensic dentists. Investigators should be aware of these rules and suggested dental protocols. They are available online at the website www.abfo.org.

SCIENTIFIC LITERATURE ON BITE MARK IDENTIFICATION

A literature review on the subject of bite mark analysis was presented at the 2000 AAFS meeting in Reno, Nevada.[1,2] The material was derived from English language publications from 1960 to 1999. One hundred and twenty written-contained studies exist of empirical testing (15%), case reports (40%), technique studies (23%), commentaries (20%), legal and literature reviews (32%). The 1970s brought out initial articles of first impression about bite mark that were later used in the judicial system to justify the consideration that bite mark analysis was scientific. The 1980s were the decade of greatest activity. The 1990s should be considered the period where biochemical analysis of salivary DNA evidence arrived as the first independent means of confirming or eliminating bite mark opinions.

The accuracy of skin as a substrate for bite marks

The bulk of bite mark cases involve injuries on skin. This is not considered a good material to record the impression of the biter.[3,4] The literature shows, however, that the bulk of experimental studies involve bite mark in inanimate materials. Skin has considerable anatomical differences (e.g. breast tissue versus other locations) and also is affected by posture and movement at the time of biting. A 1971 study[5] is the first of only two studies that describe and measured these factors.

They found both shrinkage and expansion of the skin at various positions on the body. The maximum distortion found was 60% expansion at one location. Such variability was seen that the author cautioned about the need to know the exact position of the body at the time of biting before attempting an analysis.

Uniqueness of the human dentition

Identification from bite marks is founded on the theories: (1) the dental features of the biting teeth (six upper and six lower teeth) are unique, and (2) these dental details can be transferred and recorded in the actual bite mark. This forms the basis for bite mark admissibility in court. The overall "uniqueness" of dental characteristics is a common statement used in court and in literature. This conclusion is generally accepted but is subject to considerable criticism. The reason it is criticized is that it has never been proven. The best test of a bite mark is to say that a person's teeth "could have made this bite mark". Caution must be exercised in bite mark opinions. The "probability of a mismatch" (as used in DNA results) must be calculated to inform the fact finder of the significance of connection between a subject and a bite mark. This information is not available to the dentist.

A study[6] of five sets of identical twins occurred in 1982. The separation of one twin from other by their dental characteristics was the conclusion of the paper. The authors went on to apply these findings to the general human population. A 1984 study[7] studied 384 X-ray prints of wax bites that were created and then hand traced to produce the outline of the original teeth.

This study confirms that significant variability exists in the human dentition, but not that every person's dentition is identifiable from every other person's. The authors commented in their article, "[the question is] whether there is a representation of that uniqueness in the mark found on the skin or other inanimate object".

Analytical techniques

Testing of methods is an essential basis for confidence in forensic procedures. Bite mark analysis is no exception. The wide variety of comparison techniques allowed by the ABFO is based on a consensus of the members of the organization. The array of photographic methods, bite mark and suspect exemplar production and comparison methods are generally accepted, but rarely scientifically tested. Sweet and Bowers[8] tested the relative accuracy of five generally used transparent overlay methods. Xerographic and radiographic methods are most commonly used. Their study concluded the fabrication methods utilizing the subjective process of hand tracing should be discontinued as being the least accurate.

FUTURE IMPROVEMENT TO BITE MARK IDENTIFICATION

As a number of legal commentators have observed, bite mark analysis has never passed through the rigorous scientific examination that is common to most sciences. The literature does not go far in disputing that claim. Definitive research in these areas is something for the future.

REFERENCES

1. Bowers CM. Identification from bitemarks: Literature review on bitemark identification, Section 30–2.1.6. In: David L Faigman, David H Kaye, Michael J Saks and Joseph Sanders (eds). *Modern Scientific Evidence: The Law and Science of Expert Testimony*, 2002. West Publishing Co.

2. Bowers CM, Pretty IA. Critique of the Knowledge Base for Bite mark Analysis During the '60's, '70's and Early 80's. *Proceedings of the 2000 AAFS Convention.* Reprint permission granted by ASTM, Inc.

3. Atsu SS, Gokdemir K, Kedici PS, Ikyaz YY. Bite marks in forensic odontology. *J Forensic Odontostomatol* 1998; 16: 30.

4. Stoddart TJ. Bitemarks in perishable substances. *Brit Dental J* 1973; 135: 85.

5. Devore DT. Bitemarks for identification? A preliminary report. *Med Sci Law* 1971; 11: 144.

6. Sognnaes RF, RD Rawson. Computer comparison of bitemark patterns in identical twins. *J Am Dental Assoc* 1982; 105: 449.

7. Rawson RD, Ommen RK. Statistical evidence for the individuality of the human dentition. *J Forensic Sci* 1984; 29: 245.

8. Sweet D, Bowers CM. Accuracy of bitemark overlays, comparison of five common methods to produce exemplars from a suspect's dentition. *J Forensic Sci* 1998; 43: 362.

CHAPTER 9

PHOTOGRAPHY AND FORENSIC DENTAL EVIDENCE

Photography is commonly the only means a forensic dentist can evaluate the evidence in bite mark and abuse cases. Law enforcement's reliance on photography is extremely well established and multiple protocols exist for each jurisdiction. This chapter is not meant as a substitute for these detailed narrations but hopes to emphasize aspects regarding dental evidence and focuses on the methods required for proper documentation of dental evidence. Most examples will point out problem areas in specific evidence photographs.

In many cases, people other than the forensic dentist will originate the crime scene photography. Photography is vitally important since the original evidence in homicide cases is eventually lost due to postmortem changes, burial and cremation. In live patients, injuries heal and will fade from sight. It is necessary for law enforcement to be certain that the injuries to skin and other objects are properly documented, to be reproduced for later analysis. Conventional film photography is still the best, with digital pictures being useful for backup purposes.

Dentists may take their own pictures during an autopsy to document postmortem dental features, abuse injuries and bite mark cases. Quite often, however, the dentist is *not* present and simply receives images taken by someone else. This can present limitations due:

1. Poor lighting at the scene or morgue.
2. Poor camera positioning in relation to the object photographed.
3. Lack of scale or sizing object in the frame of the photograph.
4. Misalignment of the scale, camera, and evidence which creates an irreparable distortion in the picture.

A well-taken picture far surpasses verbal or written descriptions or drawings. Bite mark analyses requires specific dimensional control of the objects being

Forensic Dental Evidence
ISBN: 0-1212-1042-1

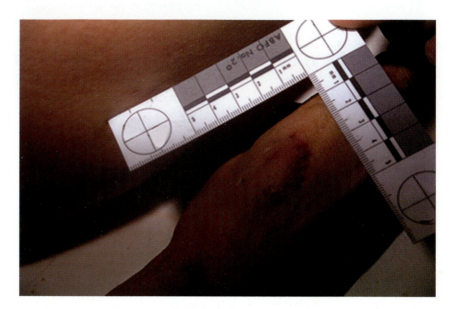

Figure 9.1

This homicide case photograph has problems of (1) camera placement, (2) the placement of the scale, and (3) poor illumination. The camera is showing a considerable off-angle (not directly above the injury) distortion. This is proven by the elliptical circular references (they should be round). The popular ABFO No. 2 scale is not placed parallel to the bruise present in the picture severely impairing its use to create a life-size picture of the injury. This image is impossible to be used as a 1:1 image as it exists.

photographed because the dentist takes life-sized models of a suspect's teeth and superimposes them onto the crime scene evidence. Figure 9.1 is an example of poor photographic technique.

OUTLINE OF PHOTOGRAPHIC DUTIES

Good photographic results are a minimum standard for every competent law enforcement agency. Poor crime scene photography will impact the quality and outcome of every forensic case and reflects negatively on everyone involved. Standardization of equipment and procedures, combined with regular training of personnel, has been proven to be the equation for acceptable results. Figure 9.2 discusses another problem with a scale's placement.

The primary purpose is to photograph evidence before it has changed or has been disturbed by third parties. The use of videotaping during an autopsy should *not* be a substitute for conventional still photography. Figure 9.3 demonstrates another example of scale misalignment.

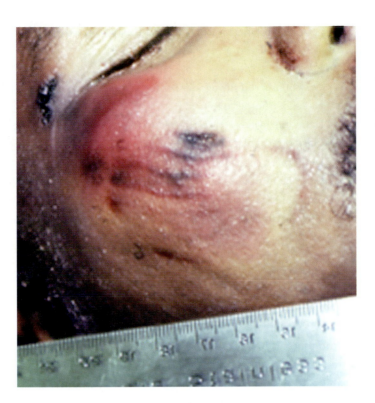

Figure 9.2
This is another picture from the bite mark case described in Chapter 3. The use of the autopsy ruler in this photograph is incorrect due to its misalignment with the injury on the cheek.

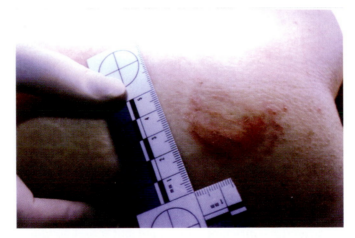

Figure 9.3
This ABFO No. 2 rule has been modified. The lower leg of the ruler has been cut off. The intact upper leg is not in the proper plane as the injury. Checking the circular reference targets proves that the ruler is misplaced. The camera placement, however, appears to be proper.

LOGGING PHOTOGRAPHS TAKEN

The courtroom use of photographs requires each document be considered "accurate and representative" of the crime scene and the object considered of evidentiary value. Proof of the photographs authenticity starts at the crime scene itself. The best way to satisfy this standard is to create a *photo log* that contains the following information:

- Case number of the agency controlling the scene and evidence.
- Name of photographer.
- Date/time when evidence is photographed and date of originating incident.
- Place where the photograph was taken.
- Description of evidence in picture.
- Equipment used – specific camera, flash type, film type, number of exposures, optical filters, settings for f-stops and lens speeds, digital image capture devices and electronic peripherals used to store and manipulate the image files.

STANDARD PHOTOGRAPHIC PROTOCOLS

DENTAL IDENTIFICATION CASES – AUTOPSY PICTURES

The first view is the front of the deceased's face as it is seen before the autopsy commences. This documents the condition of the remains when first found. The viewable body may be photographed to show later to family for possible visual identification. The second view should show the front teeth. In burn cases and decomposition cases, the facial muscles have to be dissected away. The teeth may be so carbonized that later removal during the autopsy may destroy them. If rigor has made the jaws of a viewable body impossible to open wide, waiting 12–24 hr rather than dissecting away tissue is recommended. Intraoral pictures may be taken after the jaw muscles relax or, after dissection, the jaws should be independently pictured. The jaws should be placed "in occlusion" which simulates the closing position of the teeth.

BITE MARK PHOTOGRAPHS: THE REQUIREMENTS FOR CLOSE-UP PHOTOS

An overall picture should be used to orient the injury on the person, or the location of a bitten object at a scene. During autopsy, this would be a picture showing the entire body, unwashed and therefore untouched. This establishes the unaltered condition of the evidence and only later should a picture with a case card or number be placed in the frame. Figure 9.4 should be an "orientation" view that allows the investigator to know where the anatomical location of the skin injury is.

The next step is a close-up orientation with the scale that is described in the following section. Use of both BW and color film is important. This photo will be used for forensic comparison and must accurately detail the color and

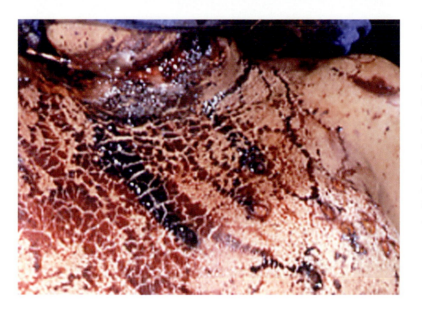

Figure 9.4
This autopsy photograph shows the condition of the homicide victim in the left chest area before cleaning the entire body. This documents the location without viewing the entire body. Later pictures will document the condition of the skin injuries in closer detail with and without the use of measurement scales.

contrasting black and white features of the physical evidence. The requirements for bite marks is similar to other areas of physical evidence photography such as:

- Fingerprints.
- Blood stain patterns.
- Gunshot residue deposits.
- Shoe prints and tire prints.
- Fracture lines in glass and other materials.

The use of natural lighting at an actual crime scene should be attempted while using oblique lighting. The autopsy room, however, usually does not allow such freedom. In that case, artificial lighting and supplementary lighting is necessary. The important step is to avoid "burning out" the bite mark with excessive direct light, flash exposure, and reflections. The use of oblique lighting (light at 45° to surface) is particularly important to allow three-dimensional (having depth) features to be highlighted as areas of light and shadow.

PROPER USE OF SCALES AND MEASURING DEVICES FOR CLOSE-UP PHOTOGRAPHY

The placement, next to the evidence, of a scale, measuring tape, or ruler is very important for later use of the photograph for forensic comparisons (Figure 9.5). The two-dimensional detail and proper size of the evidence item is dependent on the scale's ability to clearly show its linear markings and circular reference targets. Chapter 7 provides advanced information on issues relating

Figure 9.5

This picture shows a close-up view of a human bite mark. The scale chosen is the "ABFO No. 2" which is placed outside the area of the injury, but still in close proximity. Previously taken "long range" and "mid range" pictures were taken without a scale in place to show the areas now covered by the L-shaped ruler and the surrounding cloth drapes.

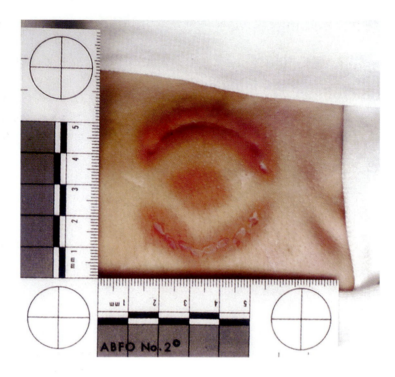

Figure 9.6

The corner of the L-shaped ruler shows the edge of the ruler close to the skin's surface. The curvature of certain bitten surfaces produce positioning problems with the camera/scale/skin alignment. Multiple pictures should be taken using sections of the bite mark to isolate the curvatures. The "circular reference target" in this picture proves that the camera is directly above the scale. Off-angle camera placement is also called "perspective distortion" that distorts the target into an ellipse. This may indicate that the evidence image is also distorted. Correction is necessary before a meaningful comparison can be made.

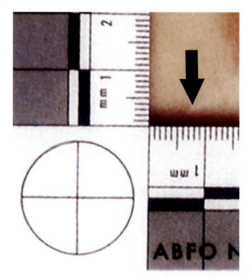

to misalignment of scales and photographic distortion. The alignment of the scale to the skin or bitten object is critical. Figure 9.6 provides a good example.

Holding the scale is commonly necessary when dealing with autopsy photos. This usually has someone doing this for the photographer. Communication between these two parties is important. Figure 9.7 is an example of an incorrect result in scale placement.

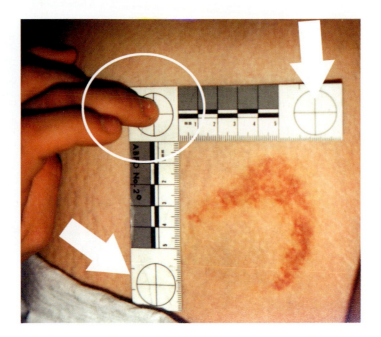

Figure 9.7

The white circle shows fingers covering a circular target reference. The remaining targets (white arrows) show effects of off-angle camera positioning. The right target is closest to the skin injury and in the correct plane. After correcting for distortion through rectification of the entire image, the right circular target can be used to reproduce the evidence image to 1 : 1.

PHYSICAL DISTORTION AND BITE MARKS

The evidence photographer must understand that skin bite marks change shape during movement during biting activity. This change is because skin is flexible and the body changes shapes as position changes. Take for example, a bite mark on a person's bicep. This upper arm muscle is quite large and moves a lot when the arm is flexed or extended out straight. The knowledge of how the arm was held during the biting allows the photographer to duplicate that position. The chances of knowing this, is low, without either a live victim or witnesses to corroborate. In the case of a deceased victim, the photographer must position the arm in multiple positions to recreate its full range of motion. For bite marks on arms, legs, breasts, buttocks, etc., the possibilities of alternative positioning should be considered. Figure 9.8 involves an evidence photo of a live victim.

Figure 9.9 shows proper placement of the camera and ruler. Unfortunately, there is another issue regarding physical distortion that still exists in the picture. Look at the picture, while ignoring the legend, and decide what the problem is with the photograph.

SUSPECT PHOTOGRAPHS

The use of color slide film and BW film is best. The ability of conventional film to reproduce high-resolution pictures outweighs the use of digital camera at the present time. Informed consent or court order is needed to perform these

Figure 9.8

The anatomy off this back is quite stable in shape, regardless of arm movement. This picture shows good placement of an L-shaped ruler below the area of injury on a back. Teeth did not cause this injury.

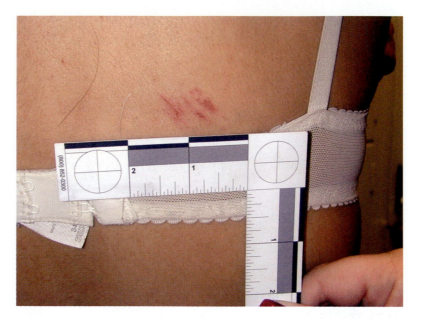

Figure 9.9

The problem is with the physical change produced by the lab assistant holding the breast. In this situation, the breast should be photographed in as many natural and assisted positions as possible. These photographs should then be digitally analyzed to consider how much shape change occurs between the various positions.

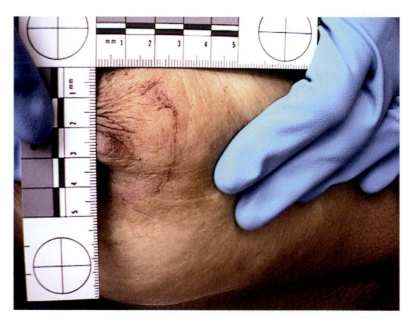

pictures. The photographs taken should be:

- Full face.
- Left profile.
- Right profile.
- Frontal picture with jaws wide open using measure.
- Close-up of upper and lower front teeth (Figure 9.10).

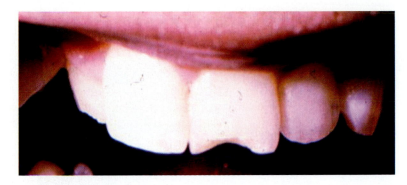

Figure 9.10
This close-up of front teeth is meant to show the chips and mal-positioning of a suspect's upper teeth.

CHECKLIST FOR FORENSIC PHOTOGRAPHY

A. USES OF CRIME SCENE PHOTOGRAPHY

1. Record the original scene and surrounding areas.
2. Record the original and unchanged appearance of physical evidence.
3. Physical comparison analysis.
4. Court testimony.

B. JUDICIAL ADMISSIBILITY OF PHOTOGRAPHIC EVIDENCE

1. Four requirements to allow a photograph into court proceedings.
   a. Object pictured must be material and relevant to the case.
   b. The photograph must not inflame emotions or tend to prejudice the court or jury against the defendant.
   c. The photograph must be free from distortion and not misrepresent the scene or the object it represents.
   d. Digital enhancements must be documented and explained.

C. PHOTOGRAPHS ARE THE ONLY WAY TO RECORD A CRIME SCENE AND ARE NOT A SUBSTITUTE FOR OTHER RECORDS. IT IS RECOMMENDED TO USE ALL OF THE BELOW TO DOCUMENT FORENSIC OBSERVATIONS.

1. Field notes.
2. Photographs.
3. Sketches.

D. FIVE STEPS IN RECORDING THE CRIME SCENE CONTAINING DENTAL EVIDENCE.

1. Secure the scene.
2. Take preliminary field notes.

Figure 9.11

This digital photograph is seriously underexposed. The skin injury is very faint and the poor lighting will require significant digital manipulation in order to restore proper color values. The better alternative would be to take more pictures with additional lighting during the autopsy.

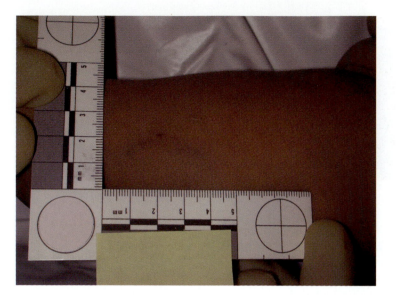

3. Take overview (long range) photographs and well as close-up pictures.
4. Make a basic sketch.
5. Record each item of evidence and its location.

E. PHOTOGRAPHS NECESSARY TO RECORD ITEMS OF DENTAL EVIDENCE

1. Take multiple photographs of each item of dental evidence.
    a. One should be an orientation (midrange) shot to show how the object or pattern is related to its surrounding context. Typically, a bite mark in skin is documented showing the location of the injury in relation to the victim's head or the nearest major anatomical location of the body.
    b. A second photograph should be a close-up to bring out the details of the object.
    c. A third photograph should include a measuring device placed in the same level (parallel to camera lens) as the injury pattern.
    d. Lighting considerations:
        ■ Block out ambient light and use a strong light source at different angles to find the light angle(s) that shows the best detail in the bite mark. Then place the electronic flash or light source at that angle when taking the photograph. Figure 9.11 is an example of poor lighting technique.

CONCLUSION

The investigator tasked with photography must be well-trained and versatile. Each case presents individual challenges that have to be understood and then overcome. As most dental (especially bite mark) evidence will disappear or degrade over time, sometimes there is only *one* opportunity to do it right. Practice (not actual casework) makes for acceptable results. The hardest failure to admit in court is that your photographs were not good enough to support the evidence you collected at a scene.

Page numbers in **bold type** refer to tables; those in *italics* to figures. Page numbers marked with an asterisk (*) indicate entries in glossary or other lists of definitions

Forensic Dental Evidence
ISBN: 0-1212-1042-1

in relation to perpetrators, in child
 abuse, 123
Violence
 bite marks, 80
 see also Abuse; Domestic violence; Sexual
 assault
Vital signs, case study, 46–47

Warren, Dr Joseph, xviii

Wax bites, 83
Wax exemplars, 83
Webster, Dr John White, xviii–xix
White, *138
Wounds
 knife/teeth, similarity between, 36, 37
 see also Injuries

X-rays, *see* Radiography